TRADING
WITHOUT
FEAR

TRADING WITHOUT FEAR

ELIMINATING EMOTIONAL DECISIONS WITH ARMS TRADING STRATEGIES

Richard W. Arms, Jr.

JOHN WILEY & SONS, INC.

New York • Chichester • Brisbane • Toronto • Singapore

Copyright © 1996 by Richard W. Arms, Jr.
Published by John Wiley & Sons, Inc.

Library of Congress Cataloging-in-Publication Data:
Arms, Richard W., 1935–
    Trading without fear / by Richard W. Arms, Jr.
        p.   cm. — (Wiley finance editions)
    Includes Index.
    ISBN 0-471-13748-0 (cloth : alk. paper)
    1. Stocks—United States—Charts, diagrams, etc.   2. Stock price
forecasting—United States.   I. Title.   II. Series.
HG4916.A717   1996
332.63'22—dc20   96-10229

Contents

Preface

Each of the technical analysis tools I invented over the last thirty years was developed to help me make better decisions for myself and (since I was then a stockbroker) for my clients. When I first conceived of the Arms Index, then known as the Short Term Trading Index, I had little idea that it would one day become so broadly used and accepted. Similarly, Equivolume was originally devised as a personal way to make better market decisions. Later, when looking for a numerical way to evaluate the principles of Equivolume, I designed the Ease of Movement calculations. As an adjunct to these methods, it became apparent that stocks are cyclical, but it appeared that the cycles conform better to a volume frame of reference than to a time frame of reference. That led to the recognition of Volume Cyclicality.

Each method led to another book, with little overlap from one book to another. In addition, each book was designed primarily as an exposition of one method and its calculation, with market strategy taking a lesser role. It has become apparent that it is time to combine the contents of those books into a single volume that blends them into a complete stand-alone method. A method that looks more to actual use of the techniques based on real trading experiences.

Technical analysis is not a static study but an ongoing search for better methods. This is particularly true of Equivolume—it is a newer method, leaving many applications still untried. In the years since its introduction a great number of new techniques have been tried; some have been adopted and many have been abandoned. One that has been found useful is the Volume Adjusted Moving Average. It appears for the first time in any book in this volume. These new techniques and applications are another motivation for writing this book.

Third, the realization of the effectiveness of some techniques and the lesser importance of others has led to new ways of applying the methods put forth in prior volumes. For example, the concept of the Power Box in Equivolume charting was perhaps implicit in the earlier books, but its importance as possibly the most significant single signal in the methodology was not emphasized or explained. This reason alone is enough to make a new book necessary.

In the pages that follow I attempt to bring together and explain all of these factors as a unified technique: the technique that I myself use to manage money. We will look at markets and stocks from many different time periods, always searching for truths—for methods which will hold up in every type of market. We will see how the methods apply in actual situations, and observe the results of their application. Proper application should lead the reader to greater profits.

TRADING
WITHOUT
FEAR

Introduction

Fear! . . . They were a group of sophisticated and prominent businessmen: bankers, attorneys, utility executives, scientists, and doctors. They acted calm and detached. They joked and discussed. But they were scared!

I was the speaker for their meeting. But it was not the usual meeting, nor would I be giving my usual luncheon speech. There would be no nodding heads in the audience, even after a drink and a meal. It was October 21, 1987. Just two days after the market had taken its biggest one-day hit in history, with the Dow industrials closing down 516 points. In the prior two days the market had traded its heaviest volume ever. Since the beginning of the month the market had dropped more than 34 percent—over 900 Dow points. True, it had regained some of the loss in the last two days, but the rally looked far from convincing. Markets continued to be chaotic.

I was told to speak to their group only the day before. The scheduled speaker had canceled at the last minute. Strange that I, a market analyst and author of books and articles on the technical aspects of the stock market, would happen to be invited to speak on this particular day. The group had never asked me to speak before.

I entered the meeting room, where the waiters were dealing out salads at the still empty tables, and went over to the "no host" bar in the far corner, where I had spotted a couple of acquaintances. As we spoke and they asked questions about the recent stock market action, I realized they were trying to act very unconcerned but were in reality deeply worried. They were not brokers and probably were not heavily committed in the market, but the stock market had suddenly made the front page of every newspaper, and it was obvious that panic was gripping Wall Street. They wondered if this was a replay of 1929. The press was calling it a crash, and they had all either experienced or heard about the Great Crash. I could sense the fear that permeated that room. It was the same fear penetrating every stock market around the world.

Later, as the dessert was served, I was introduced. "Gentlemen," I began, "There has been no crash! What we have seen is a traditional and long overdue panic. The evidence has been before us for months, but most investors have chosen to ignore it. The market has been needing exactly the medicine it has just received. Now perhaps it can start recuperating from its illness."

I went on to trace the progress of the bull market that had been in effect for five years. Being a technician I did not talk about price/earnings ratios or yields. I spoke of price movement and volume. I showed trends that accelerated into steeper trends and were then superseded by even steeper trends. I pointed to volume that increased each month, and stocks being bid up indiscriminately. I quoted from a number of my own advisory letters published over the prior few months, warning of the extremely overbought condition of the market.

I then talked about panics, crashes, and bear markets and tried to differentiate among them. *Panics* are brief and violent and usually get the job done in a hurry. They are typified by huge volume through a very wide trading range and usually come off the top of a move. They are a natural readjustment in a market which has gotten ahead of itself. *Crashes* are rather different. They come after a market has repeatedly tried to go higher and failed. They come when a market has become unsound and is in real, lasting trouble. In retrospect, they are precursors to a major economic decline, whereas panics are not. But at the time, of course, that is not known. *Bear markets* are more like a crash that happens slowly than they are like a panic. They do not seemingly come out of nowhere. They are usually preceded by a period of topping. Volume is very heavy as the market refuses to go higher, and the next step is a rolling over to the downside. Bear markets can go on for many months, as prices just continue to erode.

The market break in October 1987 looked like a panic. It came on rapidly and came from a high in the market. It was a violent convulsion, with sellers all rushing for the exits at the same time. It was a disorderly market with huge volume. In a matter of days the gains of a year were erased. The most important fact was the lack of topping action in the market. True, there had been very heavy trading for a number of months, but it had been accompanied by upward price movement. Hence, the market never indicated that it was encountering formidable and lasting resistance. Looking back at history, bull markets end by encountering insurmountable supplies of stock for sale. They try to butt their way through a barricade, and finally admit defeat and begin to slide. Crashes seem to be an accelerated version of the same scenario. That is why I told my audience that they had just witnessed a panic, not a crash.

I ended the speech by pointing out that the market is a delicate balance between fear and greed, and that those who make money are the ones who observe and use those emotions in others rather than succumbing to them. I suggested that the fear in the marketplace, and in fact in the public in general, was greatly overdone. "When everyone is greedy, that is the time to be afraid, and when everyone is afraid, that is the time to be greedy. A few months ago everyone was so greedy that they were willing to pay up indiscriminately for stocks. Now everyone is afraid and is dumping his or her holdings just as indiscriminately. It seems to me that this is a time to go against the crowd."

In this book we will talk a great deal about fear and greed. We will see how knowledge can help us avoid succumbing to those two very powerful emotions. We will learn to control those emotions in ourselves while recognizing their presence in others, and we will study methods of capitalizing on that knowledge. Fear will become our friend rather than our enemy, since it will be the emotion we see in others that leads to profits for ourselves. Greed, too, will become our ally, as we recognize its excesses in others and avoid its devastation in our own actions. Truly, we will learn to invest without fear. That is not to say we will invest without caution. Nor will we invest without the desire to succeed. We will, however, use fear and greed as attributes rather than failings. Caution is healthy, while panic is deleterious. A desire to succeed is imperative, while unreasoning avarice is delusional.

As used here, the words *fear* and *greed* should have no negative connotation. *Greed*, as I use it, merely describes the emotion that drives people to invest. *Fear* is the emotion that drives people to get rid of their investments. If the word *greed* bothers the reader, substitute *hope*.

The key to investment success, if there be just one, is the ability to remain emotionally detached. That detachment is achieved only through confidence. That confidence is arrived at only through knowledge. That knowledge is arrived at through thought, study, hard work, and experience. In this book I try to impart knowledge and experience acquired over the last thirty years. The reader will need to put in the thought and hard work. I attempt to share as much experience as possible, in order to help the reader build confidence. But the biggest confidence builder is success. The methods in this book have been successful for me. They can be for you.

This book follows a logical sequence, with each chapter building upon the chapter that precedes it. Therefore, the reader should go through it in that manner. Skipping around will be a less-effective approach than following the progression. However, the reader who is thoroughly familiar with the Arms Index, Equivolume charting and Ease of Movement may wish to skip over those chapters.

Chapter 1, I believe, is required reading for everyone, regardless of his or her market experience. It sets the stage for what follows and perhaps does more than any other chapter to make sure that the investor is confident about the effectiveness of our approach. Chapters 2, 3, and 4 deal with methodology covered in my three prior books. They explain the Arms Index, Equivolume charting, and Ease of Movement. Chapter 5 describes a newer addition to the methodology, Volume Adjusted Moving Averages. This has never before appeared in book form and has been described only briefly in one magazine article. It should not be skipped.

This book deals with technical analysis, and a specific form of technical analysis at that. It says nothing about fundamental analysis. In the next chapter we will see why that is so.

Why Technical Analysis?

Technicians usually start off as quite normal people. It is only later that they change. They start off believing that logic and hard work lead to just rewards, and that by clear and informed reasoning they will reach the land of prosperity and happiness. It is only later that they realize, if they are lucky, that logic is a pitfall and that the road to riches is paved with the bodies of those who tried to be logical. The true technician is one who has realized that the market is not logical—it is emotional. Moreover, the way to walk up that road of bodies is to become not logical but superlogical. Technicians realize that the logical are stepping-stones for those who understand the emotionalism of the marketplace and capitalize on it. When investors discover that their very systematic decisions are not acting as they theoretically should, they abandon logic in favor of emotionalism. That emotionalism is their downfall.

In this chapter I hope to convince every reader that technical analysis can lead to that type of superlogic which eliminates emotionalism and allows traders to take advantage of the emotions of others.

The trouble with fundamental stock market analysis is that it is so reasonable! It makes sense to think that a company with a good product, with good management, with good sales and earnings, will be a profitable investment. All you have to do is look around for companies that meet these criteria and you will make money by buying their stock. What could be easier? It's the classic way to invest, and it must be correct because it is so reasonable. Besides, so many people agree with you when you make your investments based upon fundamentals. You are acting in a logical and rational manner. It is a comfortable way to trade. If the price doesn't do as you expect, you can still feel secure because you own a stock with good fundamentals.

The problem is that so often stocks don't act as logically as you acted in buying them. If you can be absolutely logical and sensible in choosing a stock it seems only fair that the stock should act as sensibly and logically, and go up. But stocks don't always do that!

Technical methods are counterintuitive. The difference between *fundamental analysis* and *technical analysis* is much like the difference between Newtonian physics and quantum mechanics. When Sir Isaac Newton put forth his ideas everyone nodded and said, Oh yes, that makes sense. It is logical and can be visualized. The interdependence and interaction between all parts of the universe, from the macrocosm to the microcosm, were very comforting. This meant that every action and reaction obeys immutable laws. It fit with everyday observations. The apple falling to the ground and the rising of the sun following the same laws were comfortable concepts. They made sense; they could be diagrammed and visualized. They could be described mathematically. Even for the nonscientist, they were reassuring concepts. Immutable laws were supplanting random chance.

Then along came Heisenberg, who said that the clockwork universe is an illusion. He showed that the rules do not apply when we look at the tiniest components of the universe. There is no clockwork universe, but a universe ruled by chance. It was an uncomfortable concept and hard to accept. So unacceptable that Einstein fought the idea, uttering his famous quote, "God does not play dice!"

Technical analysis has the same drawback. It is not comfortable or easy to accept. Both technical analysis and quantum mechanics are counterintuitive concepts. But quantum mechanics was a step beyond Newtonian physics and technical analysis is a step beyond fundamental analysis. Modern scientists have had to steel themselves against the urge to try to visualize that which cannot be visualized, and have had to accept the uncomfortable mathematics which show that a wave is also a particle and that a position is not truly a position but a probability. They have had to accept the fact that the ability to know both where something is and how it is moving is blocked by the uncertainty principle. Similarly, the stock market trader must learn to accept the fact that there is a great difference between the business of a company and the market action of its stock. Successful trading requires a change in one's thinking—an acceptance of a less-comfortable methodology.

Perhaps it is because of this objectivity and lack of emotionalism that technicians are often characterized as contrarians. It often appears that they act differently than the crowd, suggesting that they always want to do the opposite of the accepted dogma. Technical analysts are intent upon recognizing the emotionalism of others without falling victims to it themselves. Fear and greed produce stock prices. Recognizing an extreme excess of fear or greed in a particular stock or commodity can mean going in the opposite direction and profiting from it. Notice, however, the words *extreme excess*. Prices are moved by emotions, so a normal preponderance of greed is the force that puts prices higher. It is only when greed forces prices to an abnormal state that one should consider becoming a contrarian. Too often it is thought that the way to success is to always behave differently than the crowd. However, much of the time the crowd is right. It is only at turning points that the crowd is wrong. Therefore, it is necessary to recognize the excesses of emotionalism rather than merely try to go contrary to the prevailing emotions.

For example, suppose a stock has been moving sideways for a long time. Each minor sideways swing reflects one side or the other trying to get the upper hand. However, neither the bulls nor the bears have the strength to generate a lasting move. It is a stock in a sideways standoff.

We see such activity in the chart of Central & Southwest in Figure 1.1. Between June and December of 1994 it was repeatedly turned back on any rally to the 23½ area and repeatedly found support around 20. Finally, at point *A* in late January of 1995 it gathered strength and moved through the resistance area with increasing volume. The balance between fear and hope had been upset in favor of hope, so the stock started

Figure 1.1 CENTRAL & SOUTHWEST—SUPPORT AND RESISTANCE

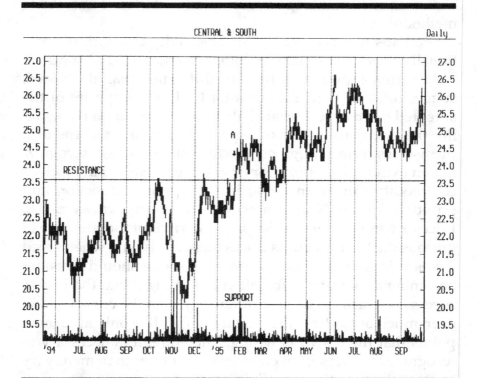

moving higher. The bulls, who represent aggressive greed in the marketplace, got control and the price started to advance. Here we see a preponderance of greed, which overwhelmed the sellers and therefore moved the price higher. A true contrarian would have to become a seller, since the emotionalism of the marketplace was on the *buy* side. Obviously a bad decision! Early in a move, and during a move, one must be a trend follower. A contrarian opinion is likely to be profitable only later in the move. It is great to "go where the crowd is coming from" at times, but only when all of the crowd seems to be moving in the same direction.

It is often said that technical analysts are lazy. It appears easier to look at a chart than to study all the fundamentals which go into a thorough analysis of a company. In terms of individual stocks, that is perhaps true. A technician with many years of experience is able to look at the chart of a single stock and quickly ascertain whether it is of interest for further study. I often look through the charts of hundreds of stocks in a short time, in order to find ones to spend more time on. It may appear easy to ask the computer to display many stocks, one after another. However, the ability to quickly spot attractive situations is acquired only after a great deal of experience.

Instead of spending large amounts of time on a single stock or industry, the technician is able to look at a much broader picture. It becomes a more universal outlook, including not just a single part of the market, but the entire market. It is for that reason that technicians are so often called upon to give broad market opinions for the media and often become spokespersons for the companies they represent.

But why does technical analysis work? It is because technical information encompasses and surpasses the fundamental considerations. In the following chapters we will not look at dividends or price/earnings ratios. Sales and profit margins will be ignored. Even the business a company is in will be largely bypassed. But that is not because these factors are thought to have no influence upon a stock—rather, it is because we do not know how much or how little a fundamental piece of information is likely to affect the price. Any piece of information—good or bad—has an effect, which is modified by a great number of other factors. Was the news anticipated? Did insiders already know about it, and if so, had they already acted upon it? Was the news really as good or bad as the company spokesperson implied? Did the news come after a long advance in the stock, or had it been in a decline? Was the stock in favor or out of favor prior to the news? Moreover, was its industry strong or weak? What about the overall market, was it in a decline or an advance? These and many other influences will greatly affect the way in which a stock's price is likely to change as a result of a piece of fundamental information. The importance of a news item is the effect it has after being filtered through the minds of millions of investors. The emotional response to the news, rather than just the news, determines its effect. The beauty of technical analysis is that it reflects that filtering process. The price and volume of a stock accurately reflect the exact valuation placed upon it by the millions of watching investors. Not only are the fundamentals reflected, but so are the emotions.

The price of a stock, therefore, contains all of the facts that are known about a company. But more than that, it reflects all of the fears and hopes of the public in view of the fundamentals, the economy, and the market. The market is very efficient at turning facts into prices, but the conversion is done through the filter of emotions. Facts affect the balance between fear and hope, and prices reflect the new equilibrium of those two emotions.

There are a great number of technical tools available, some new and some very old. We will look at only a very few tools in the following pages. However, they are and should be used as a complete methodology. *Equivolume* looks at the same information as a bar chart with volume across the lower margin, but it looks at it differently. So there is no need to also study a bar chart. *Volume cycles* allow one to estimate price objectives, thereby avoiding the need for point and figure charts. *Ease of Movement* turns the Equivolume graphics into a numerical evaluation, thereby producing an oscillator and allowing comparisons of one stock to another. *Volume Adjusted Moving Averages* replace the traditional time-based moving averages. The *Arms Index* measures the internal forces of the overall market. In the next few chapters we will look closely at each of these tools before going on to see how they can be combined to make better decisions.

The Arms Index

When I think of being really cold, a particular day comes to mind. It was a January morning in Boston, and I was walking up State Street. The temperature was probably only a little below zero, but there was a strong wind blowing straight down the street into my face as I walked the few blocks to an appointment. I don't remember ever feeling colder. The reason was not just the temperature, nor was it just the wind. It was the combination of the two—the *wind chill*. Someone looking at a thermomenter out the window and not feeling that wind could not imagine the penetrating cold until stepping outside. Someone seeing the wind speed on an anemometer but not knowing the temperature would be unaware of the iciness of that walk up State Street.

Looking at the Dow-Jones averages is much like looking at a thermometer. It tells how hot or how cold the market is, but it does not tell the *wind chill*—the effect of the winds of *volume*, either into the face or behind the back of the market. To understand the market we have to measure the underlying forces as well as taking the temperature. In this chapter we look at an index which measures those forces. Combining it with the way the market is moving is much like looking at the wind chill. It takes into account prices and also the underlying volume pressures.

That measurement is called the *Arms Index,* and it is one of the most important tools we will use. With it we will ascertain the strength of the forces which determine the future direction of the market. We will look at it as a long-term indication of market pressures, to determine whether we are in a bull or bear market and recognize how much risk there is in the long or short side of the market at any given time. It will also serve to tell us what we can expect on shorter and shorter time frames as we look at smaller and smaller moving averages. Finally, we will use it as a trading tool to help us time our market activity, even during a single day of trading.

The Arms Index was originally presented in an article in *Barron's* in 1967, and was named the *Short Term Trading Index.* As the index gained in popularity it was picked up by the various real-time data vendors, with each giving it an abbreviation, a computer code. One system called it *MKDS* while another called it *TRIN,* as an abbreviation of Short Term Trading Index. It was known by many investors, for many years, by one or another of those symbols, and eventually it was picked up on the various business television channels as TRIN.

In recent years there has been a tendency to name discoveries for their discoverers. In keeping with this, and due to the efforts of a great number of friends of the author, the index is now widely referred to as the Arms Index (AI). It appears that way in the major daily and weekly business publications, and crosses the tape on CNBC and most regional TV channels as *ARMS.*

THE CALCULATION

This is really a very simple index, designed to ascertain whether advancing stocks are receiving their share of the volume at any instant. The formula is as follows:

$$\frac{\dfrac{A}{D}}{\dfrac{AV}{DV}} = \text{Arms Index}$$

Where A is the number of stocks which are up, D is the number of stocks which are down, AV is the volume on the advancing stocks, and DV is the volume on the declining stocks.

Let us look at an example. On a recent day, part way through the session, 1,082 stocks were ahead for the day and 795 were down for the day. In addition, a number of stocks were, of course, unchanged for the day, but we are not interested in them. At the same instant we could see from our quotation equipment that 115,170,000 shares had been traded in those stocks which were up and 61,260,000 shares in the stocks which were down for the day. Again we are not interested in the volume on stocks which were unchanged for the day. Putting the numbers into the preceding equation, it looks like this:

$$\frac{\dfrac{1{,}082}{795}}{\dfrac{115{,}170{,}000}{61{,}260{,}000}} = \frac{1.36}{1.88} = .72 \qquad \text{Arms Index}$$

This is quite a bullish number. We have more stocks up than down, and we have more up volume than down volume. However, the up stocks are getting more than their share of the volume. In a standoff market the Arms Index would be 1.00. Here it is less than 1.00, which says that the ratio of advancing to declining volume is stronger than the ratio of advancing to declining stocks.

Let us look at another day. The numbers at the close were:

Advancing issues = 993

Declining issues = 887

Advancing volume = 115,970,000

Declining volume = 109,400,000

Making the calculation, we find that the first ratio is 1.12 and the second is 1.06. That produces an AI of 1.06. Looking only at the advances and declines, the market would seem strong since more stocks were up than were down. In addition, one would reach a similar conclusion looking at the volume figures since volume was heavier on the upside than on the downside. The index tells a different story, however. It says that the up stocks were not getting their share of the volume; hence the AI is over 1.00. What appeared at first to be a strong day may actually be carrying a warning: Volume is flowing toward the negative side. This may be a sign of weakness rather than a sign of strength.

Here is another example:

Advancing issues = 983

Declining issues = 881

Advancing volume = 102,780,000

Declining volume = 146,710,000

There are still more stocks up than down in this example, but now we see far more volume on the downside than on the upside. This is a dramatic example of the way in which looking only at the comparison of advances and declines can be misleading. Under the guise of an up market a great deal of stock is being dumped. The calculation produces an AI of 1.59, which means that the down stocks are getting over 50 percent more than their share of the volume.

On a normal down day the numbers might look something like this:

Advancing issues = 855

Declining issues = 1018

Advancing volume = 82,220,000

Declining volume = 121,150,000

The first ratio is .84 and the second ratio is .68, both below 1.00 and both therefore in bearish territory. Also, the first ratio is higher than the second, giving the final AI a bearish reading of 1.24. It is the sort of number one would expect in a declining market, and not one which would be considered particularly significant—at least not until it is viewed in the context of other days which surround it (but more about that later).

On another recent trading day we saw the following numbers:

Advancing issues = 898

Declining issues = 986

Advancing volume = 107,140,000

Declining volume = 100,540,000

Dividing the upper fraction we get .91, but the second computation produces 1.07. In other words, since there are more stocks down than up but more up volume than down volume, we are seeing a much stronger situation than expected. It produces an Arms Index of .85, which is well into bullish territory. The message seems to be that buyers are sneaking in under the guise of a down market.

THE LOGIC

The Arms Index measures the internal dynamics of the market. It ascertains where the volume is going and how powerful that flow is. As calculated during a trading day or at the end of the day, it indicates whether the up stocks are receiving their share of the volume and the extent to which they are or are not receiving their share of the volume. Low Arms Index numbers are good, since they show that proportionately more volume is coming into the up stocks. High AI readings indicate that the down stocks are getting the action; they are, therefore, considered bad or bearish.

When the index was first invented there was little thought that it would become a part of Wall Street methodology. Consequently, the components were used in the order they appeared on the screen of the quote machine: advances, declines, advancing volume, and declining volume. By the time it became apparent that the index would be extensively used, it was too late to change it—everyone was using it in accordance with the original calculation. It would have been worthwhile to invert it, so that big numbers would be good and little numbers bad. We are accustomed to thinking of big as better, but the index as commonly calculated says that big is worse. The calculation is done that way because it is the way that almost all of Wall Street uses it. It has become so ingrained that inverting it now would just lead to confusion. Therefore, think of it as you would a golf score—the lower the number the better.

A standoff is reached at 1.00. Values fall between .75 and 1.15 about 70 percent of the time, so that can be thought of as the normal area. When the value falls outside of that normal area it may be worth paying attention to, especially as it is compared to the way in which prices moved during the same period. Readings below .50 and above 1.75 are rare, and reflect extremes in the emotionalism of investors.

Values for the index are restricted on the low side but unrestricted on the high side. Theoretically, the index could go only from 1.00 to zero in the bullish direction but from 1.00 to infinity in the bearish direction. Consequently, lower and lower numbers are produced very grudgingly, compared to the way in which higher numbers can be generated. An easy way to compensate for this, if anyone finds it a problem, is to plot the index on semilog paper. However, after working with the index for a while and becoming familiar with its movements, compensation is really not necessary.

APPLYING THE INDEX

The index is used in two different ways: as a raw number and in a moving average. It was first developed as an intraday tool, in which only the actual reading, the raw number, was observed. (That is the number seen crossing the CNBC tape, which also appears daily in the *Wall Street Journal* and weekly in *Barrons*.) Later, however, it became evident that the index has a more far-reaching value when used in moving averages. It is that use that we will pay the most attention to in the following chapters.

Equivolume Charting

The value of the Arms Index, which we worked with in the previous chapter, is that it takes the effect of *volume* into consideration when studying market action. It is, of course, a measure of the overall market. By its very method of calculation it can apply only to the market at large. In fact, the bigger the components—that is, the more stocks listed in the index—the smoother the data, and the more reliable its signals. An Arms Index for a stock market listing only a few stocks would be extremely erratic since one or two issues with comparatively heavy trading would cause large aberrations in the index. It would be helpful to have a similar tool for individual issues. Equivolume charting is such a tool. It recognizes the fact that volume is an important consideration in the way prices move, and places volume in its proper position as an equal partner with price movement.

As trading progresses in the market (or in commodities futures, currencies, bonds, and so on), two important pieces of information are generated: (1) the price at which transactions take place, and (2) the size of the transactions. Both are equally important in the information they impart, yet the first is never forgotten and the latter is often ignored. The reason for this is simple—the price decides whether we are successes or failures while the volume is only a market measurement. If we are long a futures contract and it goes sharply higher, we are elated because we have made a shrewd investment decision. Whether it goes up on heavy trading or light trading has no effect upon our profit. Here again, we are the victims of emotions and are forgetting to be objective. While our profits and losses are the reason for our market participation, they should not cloud our ability to observe the market. The fact that the price move has produced a paper profit is certainly gratifying, but the nature of the move dictates the next decision—whether to continue to hold the position or to take the profit.

Equivolume charting makes it possible to see the role of volume in each price move more objectively, and to see the cumulative effect of volume in longer-term activity. It is a simple charting method, but one which is relatively new on the scene. It is important to realize that the method does not include anything that was not used in earlier charting methods. The market generates only the very limited technical information previously described: price and trading activity data. Equivolume provides a different way of looking at that data. It is a picture that makes the role of volume more apparent.

THE METHOD

The method is simple: Volume replaces price on the horizontal axis of the chart. The volume information that appears across the bottom margin of many bar charts is moved up into the price entry, creating a single entry that reflects both price and volume. It makes volume an equal partner with price. Each day of trading (or week if it is a weekly chart) is represented by a box (see Figure 3.1). The top of the box represents the high of the day, the bottom of the box represents the low

Figure 3.1 **EQUIVOLUME BOX**

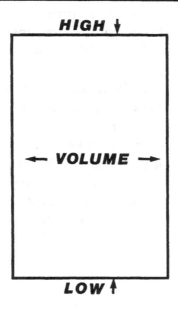

of the day, and the width of the box represents the volume traded that day.

As a result, the height of the box will vary depending upon the trading spread for the day, and the width will vary depending upon the trading activity for the day. Heavy activity spreads the box laterally and greater price movement spreads it vertically. Light volume produces a narrow box and lesser price movement produces a short box.

A day on which there is light trading but the market moves up and down through a large range will produce a tall, thin box as in Figure 3.2a. If volume is heavy and the price hardly moves it will produce a short and wide box as in Figure 3.2b. If price and volume are both fairly normal a box such as Figure 3.2c is formed for the day. A quiet trading day with a small trading range (Figure 3.2d) produces a box much like Figure 3.2c, but smaller in both dimensions. A day when the trading range is small but volume becomes heavier produces a box such as Figure 3.2e, which resembles Figure 3.2b in shape but not in size.

Each of these boxes tells its own distinct story. The shape of each box reflects how easy or hard it is for that stock to move during that particular session.

When we see a tall and thin box we know that it is taking very little effort to move the stock. Volume is light, yet price movement is large. Conversely, when we see a short and wide box we know that the stock is having difficulty progressing. A great deal of energy, expressed as volume, is being expended, but there is no movement. It is a standoff between buyers and sellers.

Figure 3.2 **EQUIVOLUME BOXES ILLUSTRATED**

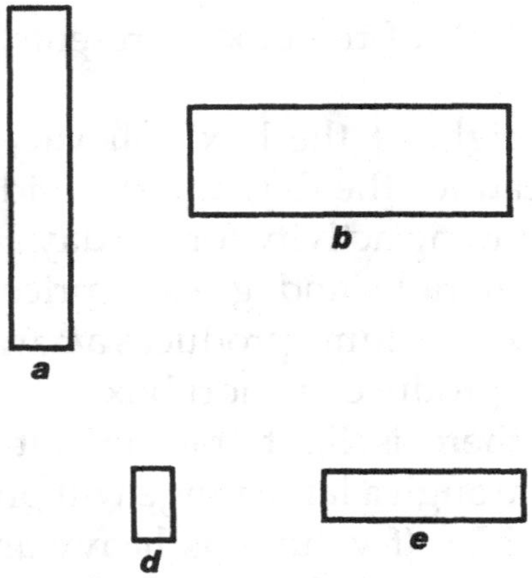

A TYPICAL CHART

Let us look at an Equivolume chart (Figure 3.3) to see how the shapes, sizes, and location of the boxes can impart information to us.

In this chart, a real chart for Adobe Systems, we are looking at only a brief time span. As we go on we will normally look at longer histories of stocks. Here we have enlarged a segment of a longer chart in order to concentrate on the details. The price scale is seen along the right margin. As on a bar chart, the top of the posting is the high for the day, and the bottom is the low for the day. For example, on Day 9 the

Figure 3.3 **EQUIVOLUME CHART—ADOBE SYSTEMS**

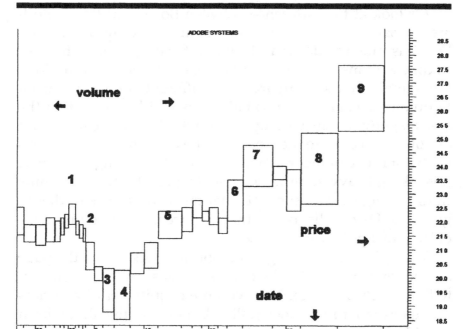

high was 27⅝ and the low was 25¼. We determine that by comparing the top and bottom of the box to the price scale. Across the bottom of the chart is the date, in this case late March and early April. In order to facilitate this study, numbers have been placed on a few of the days—not a normal practice.

The factor which makes this method uniquely informative is that the horizontal dimension represents *volume* rather than *time*. Each box on this chart represents one day of trading, with its height the difference between the high and low for the day and its width the trading volume for the day. But compare the boxes! The two boxes just before Box 1 are very small, while Box 9 is extremely large. They are each just one day of trading, but obviously Day 9 is a much more important day.

Or look at the difference between Box 6 and Box 7. Both are the same height, so they had similar trading ranges, but Day 7 is much wider than Day 6, reflecting a much heavier trading volume on that day. On a bar chart both would look the same, yet they impart very different messages on an Equivolume chart. Day 6 is tall for its width, saying that the stock is moving fairly easily—it is not taking a great amount of volume to change the price. On the other hand, Day 7 tells us that it is becoming much more difficult to change the price. It is taking heavy volume to move the price through the same trading range. Day 6 suggests that the advance has farther to go, while Day 7 tells us that the advance is running into difficulty, and a pullback is likely.

Let us look at the progression of the stock across the page and learn the story the box shapes, sizes, and locations are telling us. Prior to Box 1 the volume is quite heavy as prices move lower. At 1 the stock rallies, but only to the old highs. It is evidently trapped in a trading range and drifts down to the bottom of that range on light volume for three days. Then, at Box 2 the low of the range is penetrated with a day on which volume is heavier and price range is wider. When a stock goes down through an old area of support with increasing volume and a widening spread, it is a sign of weakness. The move down to 3 is therefore no surprise.

At 3 we see heavy volume but a wide price range, and it is a sharp downward move. That gives it the appearance of fearful selling. When fear takes over and produces such a box it is often a sign that the decline has run its course. Day 4 again shows heavy volume, but the downward move seems to have been halted. The shape of the box is similar to that of Day 3, but the stock does not go appreciably lower. This is certainly a clue that a turn to the upside may be developing, but it is still too early to be a buyer.

The next three days are very interesting, in that volume is heavy as the stock moves up. Prior to this time volume has tended to get heavier on declines and lighter on advances. After Day 4 the reverse seems to be true. For a change volume is going to the upside of the stock, adding to the evidence that a turn may be developing. Day 5 is a very square posting. The box is about as wide as it is high, saying that it is finding further upside movement to be difficult. Also, the stock has reached the highs we saw at Box 1, an obvious resistance area. When a stock starts to go square it represents a stalling of the current move and suggests that a pullback is likely. That is even more true when it occurs at an old level of resistance. Until that level is decisively overcome, the potential for a sizable profit from buying the stock does not seem likely.

After moving sideways for a number of days, the price suddenly jumps up through resistance on Day 6, with heavier volume. That box is the most important box on the page. Volume and range both increase as the stock moves up through the old level of resistance. It is what we will call a *power box* and is the most important entry we can see on a chart. It represents a change in attitude—buyers are willing to pay up for the stock and are eager to accumulate a lot of it.

The box at 7 is again more square, indicating resistance and suggesting a pullback. However, it is not at an old resistance area and is therefore not particularly worrisome. The box at 8 is another sign of strength, as the high at 7 is overcome with power. That leads to the continuing strength at Box 9. In this example we see a stock that was drifting lower, then built a base, and finally broke out to the upside with increasing volume. It is the sort of picture we always want to be looking for. Equivolume charts have told a story that would have been much harder to read on a bar chart.

In Figures 3.4 and 3.5 we see the two different ways of looking at the same information: the traditional way and the Equivolume way. We are seeing a little over half a year of the history of Alza Corp., from late 1994 and early 1995. This

Figure 3.4 **BAR CHART—ALZA CORP.**

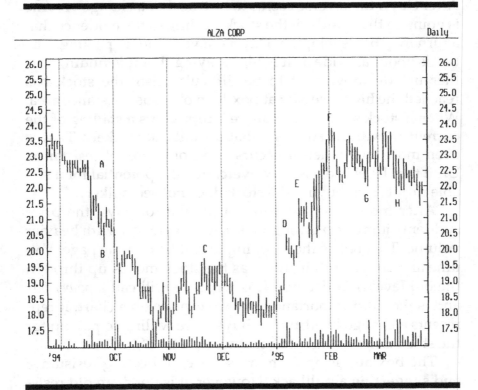

stock was selected from among many stocks that are neither small and obscure nor extremely large and active. A small stock with very little trading sometimes produces a chart that is erratic, whereas a very widely traded issue tends to produce a chart in which most of the Equivolume boxes have quite similar widths. Neither of these traits produces a drawback to the charting method, but an intermediate stock, in terms of activity, is likely to produce a chart which is easy to study because there is a large variety in box sizes without erratic behavior.

Looking first at Figure 3.4, we see a typical bar chart with each posting representing a single day of trading. Note that

Figure 3.5 **EQUIVOLUME CHART—ALZA CORP.**

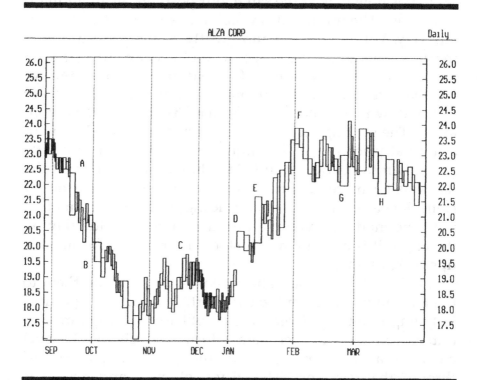

the bars are of different lengths, depending on the price range through which the stock traded. Along the bottom margin of the chart is the volume. It is possible but difficult to equate a particular day with its volume. Sometimes the combination of the price move and the volume are fairly obvious, as at the long line to the left of A. The fact that the stock has moved rapidly downward out of a sideways area, and that it did so on heavy volume, is apparent. Often, however, it is not so easy to see what effect volume is having on a particular entry, as at B or C. The entry labeled F is of particular interest because the volume is not especially heavy, making it look like just another day of trading. One is not aware that the trading range has narrowed and that the stock may be encountering resistance. An Equivolume chart solves that problem.

Let us now look at the same four postings on an Equivolume chart. The trading at A was, as we suspected, an important day. Volume did expand greatly as the price dropped through a wide trading range. As on the bar chart, it is seen that a decisive penetration of the support of the sideways area has been made. The tall but wide box is a sign of power to the downside, and suggests that the stock will now go lower. The postings at B and C are lighter-volume days with a normal price range. The Equivolume chart tells us little more than the bar chart did. At F, however, we see that the day was far more important than we would have surmised from the bar chart. The small trading range in combination with the moderate volume produces a short, wide day on the chart. It is a sign that the stock has run into formidable upside resistance.

Looking at the other labeled boxes, and relating them to the matching entries on the bar chart, D is seen as a particularly important day. After a period of base building throughout November and December, during which the 20 level emerged as a stopping point, the price jumps upward through that resistance. The heavy volume is apparent, as is the breakaway gap. However, on the Equivolume chart one immediately becomes aware that the range is narrow after the gap. The stock is encountering resistance, a clue that it is likely to pull back, thereby providing an opportunity to buy it at a better price. That happens in the next four days, and the price comes right back down to the breakout level—a very appealing time to buy the stock.

As we will see in later chapters, the stock has fulfilled the important requirements for a buy: It has completed a decline, built a base, and shown strength. That show of strength is the increase in volume on the breakout.

Box E is a further sign of strength. It penetrates the square box at D with a wide spread and heavy trading—a power box to the upside. The upward move to the high at F is signaled by that power box, and the time to take the profit is suggested by the square entry as the stock encounters resistance.

Looking at the entire chart, we can also see how the box shapes and sizes give an impression of the trend of the stock. In the first two months each downward move is accompanied by heavier trading, and each upward rally is made on lighter volume. The widths of the boxes quickly relay that information: Volume becomes heavier in the direction of the trend. Across the base, during the next two months, volume is about the same in both directions. Since there is no direction to the stock, there is little volume bias. Going into January, however, the volume tends to become heavier on advances, providing a clue that the eventual breakout from the trading area is more likely to be up than down. After the breakout the volume is consistently heavier on up moves than on down moves, informing us that the trend is up. Finally, after point F the volume tends to increase on declines, as at G and H, telling us that the next move of consequence is likely to be down.

One more thing should be noticed on this chart: the nontime x axis. On the bar chart each of the months is of the same approximate width, as seen by the time scale across the bottom. On the Equivolume chart they are not the same width, because we have substituted volume for time. January, for example, is about three times as wide as December, because volume became very heavy in January. This is a point which becomes very important in later chapters. It is the central concept to Equivolume: The market operates as a function of volume, not as a function of time. Time is a human measurement, while volume is a trading measurement.

Interestingly, this method of depicting market activity, in which price is replaced by volume on the horizontal axis was found to be an idea which had been around before. Only after a number of years of working with it, and naming it Equivolume, did I become aware that a gentleman named Edwin S. Quinn used the same technique in the late 1940s. He published a service called Investographs, in Rochester, New York.

As will be seen in later chapters, Equivolume chart interpretation can be used for stocks, futures, currencies, bonds, or any other traded instruments for which price range and volume are available. In addition, we will see how helpful they can be in recognizing trends in the market indices. First, however, we need to look at a method of reducing the Equivolume information to a numerical equivalent called *Ease of Movement*. That is the subject of the following chapter.

Ease of Movement

Ease of Movement is a method of reducing the information in an Equivolume chart to a numerical equivalent. It has the advantage of complete objectivity, in that a precise value can be established for each entry. That leads to the ability to manipulate the numbers and develop exact, unequivocal signals. The gain in precision is traded for the loss of a visual "feel" for the way the stock is trading, however. Consequently, Ease of Movement should not be used as a stand-alone tool, but as an adjunct to the Equivolume chart from which it is generated.

Each Equivolume entry contains three important pieces of information. All of them must be taken into consideration if we are to place a numerical value on each box. They are: (1) the price range for the period, (2) the volume for the period, and (3) the price change from the prior entry. We need to know how much stock traded and at what price, but we also need to place that entry in context by relating it to the price of the stock prior to that entry. We saw on the Equivolume charts in the previous chapter that the size and shape of each box tells a story—a story of the supply and demand balance affecting the stock. A square box, for example, indicates that the stock is having difficulty moving. Only by looking at what has gone before can we say that it is having difficulty moving up or down. The shape and size of the entry is meaningful only in the context of the other boxes on the chart. In addition, it is important to know how dramatic a move is involved. A price move out of a trading range is far more important than a similarly shaped box which is within a trading range. Therefore, it is necessary to observe not only the direction of the move but its extent. These are the factors, then, that must be quantified if we are to have a numerical valuation of our Equivolume chart entries.

BOX RATIO

We have seen that the shape of each box in an Equivolume chart tells us a story about the supply and demand picture for that stock. The box has a length and a width, determined by the price spread and the volume. Let us combine these into a single piece of information. We could multiply one by the other and determine the area of the box, but then we would be placing more emphasis on the size of the box than on its shape. In fact, the shape would not be directly represented, since a tall and narrow box would have the same area as a short and wide box—but on an Equivolume chart they would have very different interpretations. Instead, we will divide one by the other, and thereby produce a ratio that expresses the shape of the box. By dividing the width of the box by its height we produce a number that is smaller for tall boxes and larger for wide boxes.

For example, if a box were four units high and one unit wide, as in the first example in Figure 4.1, it would have a box ratio of 1 divided by 4 or .25. A day on which there was quite heavy volume, as in the second example, might be as high as it is wide, thereby producing a box ratio of 1.00 (3 divided by 3), and a day on which there was very heavy trading and very little price range might be one increment tall and three increments wide, producing a box ratio of 3 divided by 1, or 3.00.

Figure 4.1 **BOX RATIO**

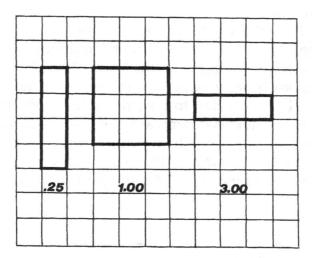

In this way we have reduced two of our critical pieces of information to a single number, which expresses their relationship to one another. The box ratio is simply the width of the box divided by its height, which means, of course, its volume divided by its spread. We will use this in a later calculation, but first let's look at the third factor we need to measure.

MIDPOINT MOVE

To place each box in context with its neighbors we need to ascertain the direction and extent of the change in price. This is done by measuring from the center of one entry to the center of the following entry. Notice that we are not looking at the close-to-close change that is printed in the newspaper. Since we are evaluating the boxes, we must look at each box in its entirety. The number we wish to ascertain is called the *mid-point move*. It is the distance from the center of one entry to the center of the next entry.

Let us look at Figure 4.2. The first entry is a day with a trading high of 20 and a low of 19. The midpoint of that box, halfway between the high and the low, is 19½. The midpoint of the next box is halfway between a low of 18 and a high of 20, or 19. Therefore, day to day, the price move from one midpoint to the next is downward from 19½ to 19, or a midpoint move of minus one-half point (−.50). The next entry has a high of 21 and a low of 19, so the midpoint is 20. Since the prior midpoint was 19, this is an upward midpoint move

Figure 4.2 **MIDPOINTS**

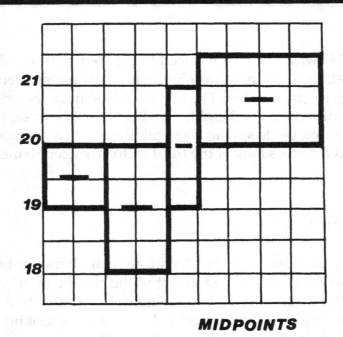

MIDPOINTS

of one point (+1.00). In the next entry the midpoint is 20¾, so the move is again a positive move from 20 to 20¾, or +.75.

Now we have valued the amount the price moved and the direction it moved. The actual formula for arriving at the midpoint is:

$$MP = \frac{(high + low)}{2}$$

and the midpoint move is:

MPM = today's midpoint − yesterday's midpoint

EASE OF MOVEMENT CALCULATION

Now that we have placed a numerical value to the three important factors, all we need to do is combine them in a logical manner. The formula we use for Ease of Movement follows:

$$EMV = \frac{MPM}{BR}$$

That is, the Ease of Movement value is derived by dividing the midpoint move by the box ratio. In this way, then, a high box ratio number, caused by a square box, produces a smaller Ease of Movement number. It signifies that the price is having trouble changing. Conversely, a tall, thin day on the Equivolume chart is represented by a low box ratio and, therefore, if the midpoint move stays the same, produces a higher Ease of Movement value. If the box ratio stays the same, a large midpoint move has a greater effect upon the Ease of Movement value, while a small midpoint move has a lesser effect on the Ease of Movement. In other words, the Ease of Movement varies directly with changes in the mid-point move and inversely with changes in the box ratio.

The preceding sections are meant as an explanation of the reasoning and logic behind Ease of Movement. To be useful, however, it needs to be normalized by expressing each part of the equation as a percentage of normal trading for the particular stock, bond, commodity, or index being studied. Although I explained the mathematics of that normalization in a prior book, it is so complex as to be almost prohibitive without the use of a computer. Fortunately, computer programs now make such calculations in an instant and display them on charts. I use the program included in the Metastock analysis product distributed by Equis, Salt Lake City. Persons wishing to delve deeper into the mathematics might wish to read my earlier book entitled *Volume Cycles in the Stock Market.* For the purposes of this discussion, however, we will look at computer-generated charts.

SMOOTHING THE RESULTS

Let us first look at the results of the Ease of Movement calculation without any smoothing (Figure 4.3).

Here we see a daily based bar chart of GTE Corp. (bottom) and the unsmoothed Ease of Movement (top). About all we can observe here is that the Ease of Movement appears to be swinging farther in both directions when the stock is in trend than it does when the stock is moving sideways. Other than that, it is such an erratic series of numbers as to have no predictive value. If one were to buy the stock each time the Ease of Movement moved into positive territory and sell it each time it moved into negative territory, the result would obviously be a great number of trades and probably little or no profit. Only the broker would be happy.

Figure 4.3 **GTE CORP. AND EASE OF MOVEMENT—
UNSMOOTHED**

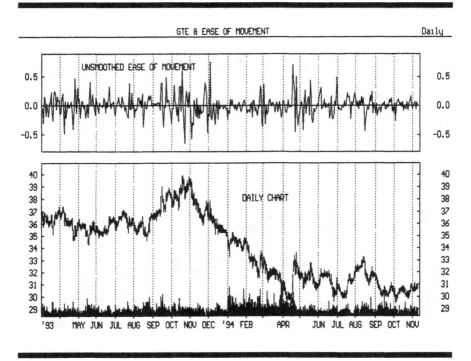

If these numbers contain a worthwhile message, we will have to do some smoothing of the data. Let us look at what happens if we combine the entries with a simple arithmetic moving average (Figure 4.4).

In this example we have done a 25-day moving average of the same data and plotted it above the price history. As can be seen, we now have an oscillator. It tends to go up when the stock goes up and down when the stock goes down. When it lingers above the zero line the stock is usually in an uptrend and when it is holding below the zero line the stock is usually in a downtrend. During trends, therefore, it is very helpful. The sideways consolidations in the stock lead to many whipsaws in the Ease of Movement average, however. Note,

Figure 4.4 **GTE CORP. AND EASE OF MOVEMENT—
SMOOTHED**

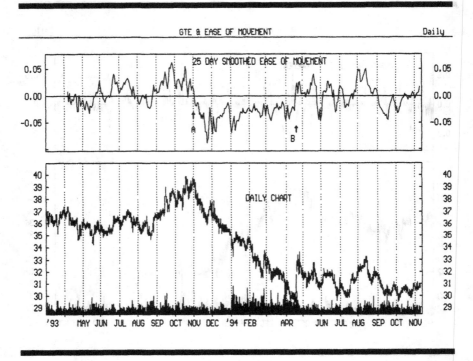

though, that even though this indicator is smoothed with over a month of trading, it is not lagging the price as we would expect. A moving average of the price tends to have a lag which is exactly a function of its length of smoothing. Ease of Movement contains price but is modified by volume and price spread, thereby becoming more effective in staying coincident. That is because the volume and spread characteristics are different at turning points than they are during trends. The mathematics of calculating the Ease of Movement helps to recognize that change in character.

Points *A* and *B* are very good signals and come in as the stock changes direction. Shorting the stock on the first signal and covering on the second signal would have been quite profitable. However, there are still a large number of other crossovers which are not as effective. It appears that a longer-term moving average may be better. We must realize, however, that we will lose some of the timeliness of the signals as we shift out to longer-term moving averages. On the other hand, we will expect to have fewer trades and stay in positions longer.

If we move out to a 50-day Ease of Movement, as in Figure 4.5, we start to see far fewer trades, and positions are of longer duration. That reduces commission costs. As can be seen, however, there are still a number of unprofitable crossovers,

Figure 4.5 **GTE CORP. AND EASE OF MOVEMENT— 50-DAY SMOOTHED**

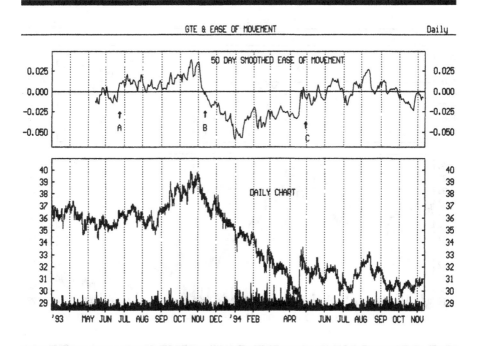

in addition to two very worthwhile trades—a long position at point *A* and a short position at point *B*.

Finally, let's look at the same stock, but this time with a 100-day moving average of the Ease of Movement (Figure 4.6).

Notice that we have greatly reduced the number of trades, so that we are tending to trade only the major moves. At the last part of the chart there are some whipsaws, but the two earlier trades are very successful. It appears that the longer-term moving average is more helpful than the short-term moving averages.

Figure 4.6 **GTE CORP. AND EASE OF MOVEMENT—100-DAY SMOOTHED**

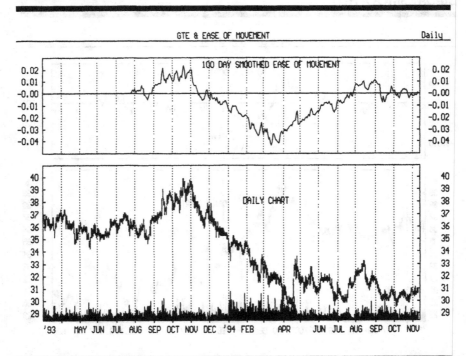

OPTIMIZING THE EASE OF MOVEMENT

Over the years I have worked with and done studies on a great number of different moving averages of the Ease of Movement, in order to arrive at the levels which seem to provide the maximum reliability and the minimum whipsaws. Now, however, using computer programs makes it a far less tedious job. A part of the program referred to earlier in this chapter makes it possible to test a great number of possibilities rather rapidly.

I asked the computer to look at all the possible moving averages between 1 and 125 and ascertain what profits would accrue if one blindly bought on each positive crossover and covered the long position on the crossover back into negative territory. This, of course, was based upon the chart of a particular stock.

The results were interesting but far from conclusive. However, by repeating the process many times on many randomly selected stocks, a pattern began to emerge. That pattern of optimum levels on the Ease of Movement showed peaks at very much the same level, regardless of the stock being studied. The following example is rather typical. Its best levels of profit are about where they were seen to occur in the majority of stocks examined.

The stock happens to be Knight-Ridder and the time period is a four-year span, using a daily based chart. Over that four-year period the stock had a number of swings in both directions, but ended up almost exactly where it began. A $1,000 investment held throughout the period, with no trading, would have lost $6.47. On the other hand, the same hypothetical $1,000 would have had widely varying profits or losses, depending upon the Ease of Movement signal followed.

In Figure 4.7 we see the distribution of profits at every Ease of Movement value from 1 to 100. The various Ease of

Figure 4.7 **KNIGHT-RIDDER—PROFIT AT ALL EASE OF MOVEMENT VALUES**

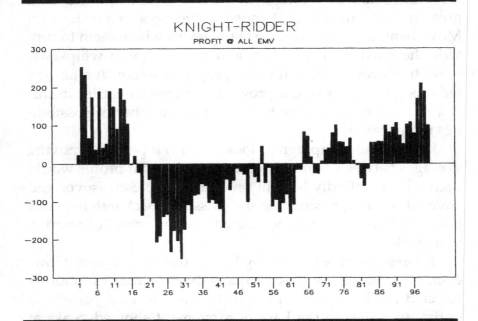

Movement levels progress upward across the bottom of the chart. The center line is the break-even point, and the height or depth of each bar represents the profit or loss one would have realized over the entire four years by blindly following every single long trade signaled by the Ease of Movement. It appears, from this graph, that the best profits are seen in the very low and very high Ease of Movement levels, with another good area around the 73 to 75 Ease of Movement zone. At the best points the profits on $1,000 are over $250. On the other hand, the levels around 30 produce losses of about the same amount.

These results are a bit misleading, however. Recall that we found earlier that lower Ease of Movement moving averages produce far more signals. Figure 4.8 shows the number of trades generated at each Ease of Movement moving average level. There are 148 different long positions entered and closed when the moving average is 1, whereas there are only 9 when the moving average is 100; and there is a very steady decline in the trade count as the moving averages become larger. Commissions would eat you up at the low Ease of Movement levels.

By dividing the profits at each level by the number of trades at each level we derive the average profit per trade at each level. That is a far more informative way of looking at the results (Figure 4.9).

Figure 4.8 **KNIGHT-RIDDER—TRADE COUNT AT ALL EASE OF MOVEMENT VALUES**

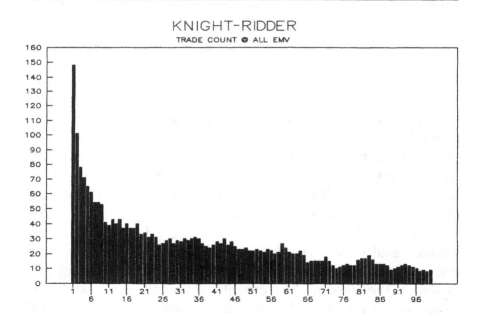

Figure 4.9 **KNIGHT-RIDDER—PROFIT/TRADE AT ALL EASE OF MOVEMENT VALUES**

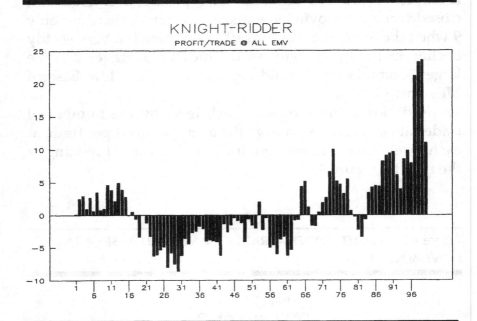

Now we see that the best results come in at two levels: around an Ease of Movement of 75 and around 98. This is consistent with the results from many other stocks. Some, of course, showed far larger profits, with the results on this stock being mediocre. Most, however, delivered the best profits in the same areas, around 75 and around 100.

The preceding work is all based upon daily charts. Very similar results are derived on a weekly chart. Since each posting on the weekly chart represents five days of trading, the peaks in the Ease of Movement optimization are at levels which are one-fifth of the preceding results—that is, around 15 and 20.

APPLYING EASE OF MOVEMENT

Looking at the preceding example, one is tempted to follow such a program—blindly trading in accordance with an optimized Ease of Movement crossover. Although it is certainly a powerful tool, we will see in future chapters that it is best used *as a tool*, not as a single discipline. We have found the optimum levels in order to refer to them in later work. They will be very helpful, but will be used in conjunction with the other tools at hand.

Volume Adjusted
Moving Averages

Stock or commodity prices are always erratic. They have rapid up and down movements that have little to do with the longer-term trend, but that can be misleading and lead to bad decisions. A traditional tool used by technicians to get around the problem is the *moving average*. It is designed to smooth the price gyrations sufficiently that the investor can trade the trends rather than the ripples. It helps the trader to avoid meaningless whipsaws and tends to lead to less-frequent trades.

SIMPLE MOVING AVERAGE CALCULATIONS

Let us look at a typical moving average calculation. In Figure 5.1 we see the closing prices of a stock over a month and a half period. Moving averages can be based upon the closes, as here, or the high, the low, or the median price. The third column shows the five-day moving average. It is nothing more than the sum of the last five closes, divided by five. The calculation is repeated each day, adding in the last day's data and dropping off the data from six days ago. This gives a simple 5-day moving average with each day having equal weight

Figure 5.1 CALCULATING THE MOVING AVERAGE

Date	Close	5-Day	10-Day
June 1	23.125		
June 2	23.75		
June 3	23.25		
June 4	24		
June 5	24.5	23.725	
June 8	25.175	24.135	
June 9	25.125	24.41	
June 10	25.175	24.795	
June 11	25.375	25.07	
June 12	25.125	25.195	24.46
June 15	24.875	25.135	24.635
June 16	24.25	24.96	24.685
June 17	24.5	24.825	24.81
June 18	24.125	24.575	24.8225
June 19	23.25	24.2	24.6975
June 22	23.125	23.85	24.4925
June 23	22.75	23.55	24.255
June 24	22.125	23.075	23.95
June 25	22	22.65	23.6125
June 26	21.875	22.375	23.2875
June 28	21.75	22.1	22.975
June 29	21.125	21.775	22.6625
June 30	19.75	21.3	22.1875
July 1	19.5	20.8	21.725
July 2	19.125	20.25	21.3125
July 6	19.75	19.85	20.975
July 7	20.25	19.675	20.725
July 8	20.375	19.8	20.55
July 9	20.25	19.95	20.375
July 12	19.25	19.975	20.1125
July 13	18.75	19.775	19.8125
July 14	18.5	19.425	19.55
July 15	18.125	18.975	19.3875
July 16	18.75	18.675	19.3125

in the moving average. The fourth column shows a similar calculation, but for a 10-day moving average.

In Figure 5.2 we see how the price and two of the moving averages appear on a chart. The trace that starts the farthest to the left is the actual closing price of the stock on each day, marked with small squares and connected by lines. The trace that starts slightly to the right of the price and is marked with small *x*s is the 5-day moving average. Note how it follows the price line very closely but is much smoother. In addition, it is obvious that it turns down later than the price in mid-June, and is also late on the brief rally in early July. That lateness is characteristic of a moving average. The more the price is smoothed, the later the turns occur—leading to late *buy* and *sell* signals. It is the price paid for the smoothing.

Figure 5.2 **MOVING AVERAGES—SIMPLE, 5-DAY, AND 10-DAY**

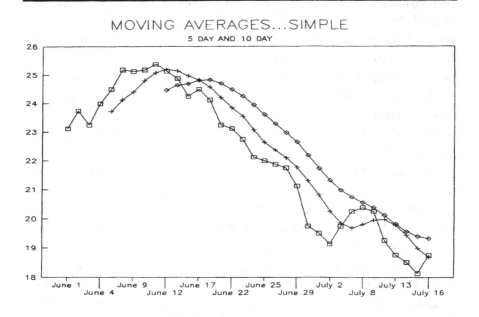

The third line on the chart is the 10-day moving average. It is even smoother, not even reacting to the rally in early July. As with the 5-day, it is late in signaling the top in mid-June. Because of its smoothness it helps avoid an attempt to trade the small rally, which would be costly.

We see here two ways that moving averages can be used as a trading tool. By watching when the 5-day moving average line crosses the closing price line one would sell soon after the top is made, cover the decline with a good profit at the time of the small rally, and then lose money on the whipsaw created by that rally. If, instead, one watched the 10-day and its relationship to the price line, a short would be initiated a bit later, and the position would stay on for the remainder of the time in the example. Using the 10 would, in this case, sacrifice a bit of the profit at the beginning of the decline, but avoid the whipsaw.

The third way of using these two moving averages is to trade when one moving average crosses the other. Because both moving averages lag the actual price, the signal comes in even later than the 10 versus price crossover. Again, the tardiness of the signal costs a little on initiating the short position, but the whipsaw is avoided. In later chapters we will look at two moving averages and the crossovers they generate. That method is worthwhile even if a very short-term moving average is used for one of the two lines, because it reduces the range of the prices to a single line and therefore creates unequivocal crossovers.

As alluded to previously, the largest drawback to moving averages is the fact that they are late, and the smoother they are the later the signals they generate. The most common method designed to get around the problem is to weight the entries so that more recent information has a larger influence on the prices. This has both advantages and drawbacks. The signals are a bit earlier, but the most recent information, being overemphasized, can more easily create false signals. Another method, the one we will use, is Volume Adjusted Moving Averages.

If, as we observed in the chapter on Equivolume charting, the market seems to move in a volume frame of reference rather than a time frame of reference, then it would seem logical to use moving averages that adhere to the same principles. If volume, rather than time, is how change occurs, then we need to assign a volume rather than a time parameter to our moving averages.

CALCULATION OF VOLUME ADJUSTED MOVING AVERAGES

Since some boxes on an Equivolume chart are wider than others, because they represent heavier trading, why not let them have a larger effect upon our moving average? Suppose that we give the smaller-volume days a value of one, and any heavier-volume days a larger value, depending upon how many multiples of that volume number trade on a given day. If, for example, we assume that on a light trading day in a particular stock 10,000 shares change hands, then we would assign a single volume increment to each 10,000 shares or any part thereof. It is exactly the same method we used to decide how wide to plot the boxes on the Equivolume charts. We then let each box contribute as many entries to the moving average as it is wide. A day of over 20,000 shares would be three times the basic width, so it would become three entries of our moving average. On a 10-entry moving average that one day would contribute 30 percent weight to the moving average while a light day of under 10,000 shares would contribute only one entry, or 10 percent, to the moving average.

In Figure 5.3 we have adjusted the volume on the preceding example. Now we have a longer table because some of the days are more than one volume increment wide. On June 2 over 10,000 but under 20,000 shares traded, so we assign it a volume increment of two. That necessitates giving that day double weight in our moving average. Therefore, we have

Figure 5.3 CALCULATING VOLUME ADJUSTED MOVING AVERAGES

Date	Close	Volume	10-Interval	20-Interval
June 1	23.125	2		
June 2	23.75	2		
	23.75			
June 3	23.25	1		
June 4	24	1		
June 5	24.5	2		
	24.5			
June 8	25.375	4		
	25.375			
	25.375		24.300	
	25.375		24.525	
June 9	25.125	5	24.663	
	25.125		24.800	
	25.125		24.988	
	25.125		25.100	
	25.125		25.163	
June 10	25.25	6	25.238	
	25.25		25.225	
	25.25		25.213	
	25.25		25.200	24.750
	25.25		25.188	24.856
	25.25		25.200	24.931
June 11	25.375	3	25.225	25.013
	25.375		25.250	25.119
	25.375		25.275	25.188
June 12	25.125	3	25.275	25.219
	25.125		25.263	25.250
	25.125		25.250	25.238
June 15	24.875	2	25.213	25.213
	24.875		25.175	25.188
June 16	24.25	1	25.075	25.131
June 17	24.5	2	25.000	25.100
	24.5		24.913	25.069
June 18	24.125	1	24.788	25.019
June 19	23.25	1	24.575	24.925
June 22	23.125	2	24.375	24.825
	23.125		24.175	24.719

Figure 5.3 (*continued*)

Date	Close	Volume	10-Interval	20-Interval
June 23	22.75	3	23.938	24.594
	22.75		23.725	24.469
	22.75		23.513	24.344
June 24	22.125	2	23.300	24.188
	22.125		23.063	24.031
June 25	22	1	22.813	23.863
June 26	21.875	2	22.588	23.688
	21.875		22.450	23.513
June 28	21.75	1	22.313	23.344
June 29	21.125	2	22.113	23.144
	21.125		21.950	22.944
June 30	19.75	3	21.650	22.688
	19.75		21.350	22.431
	19.75		21.113	22.206
July 1	19.5	1	20.850	21.956
July 2	19.125	1	20.563	21.688
July 6	19.75	1	20.350	21.469
July 7	20.25	4	20.188	21.319
	20.25		20.038	21.175
	20.25		19.950	21.031
	20.25		19.863	20.906
July 8	20.375	3	19.925	20.788
	20.375		19.988	20.669
	20.375		20.050	20.581
July 9	20.25	3	20.125	20.488
	20.25		20.238	20.400
	20.25		20.288	20.319
July 12	19.25	2	20.188	20.188
	19.25		20.088	20.063
July 13	18.75	1	19.938	19.944
July 14	18.5	2	19.763	19.813
	18.5		19.575	19.750
July 15	18.125	3	19.350	19.669
	18.125		19.125	19.588
	18.125		18.913	19.519
July 16	18.75	2	18.763	19.500
	18.75		18.613	19.450

listed the price for that day twice. When we do a Volume Adjusted Moving Average, that day will contribute two entries to the moving average. Looking down to June 10, we see that it is listed six times. That is because volume was very heavy on that day, with at least 50,000 but not 60,000 shares changing hands. In any moving average we use, that day will contribute six parts to the moving average.

Now we can do the moving average calculation, but this time it will be a Volume Adjusted Moving Average. We will not use the same moving average parameters because we are dealing with a lot more entries for the time being studied. We know that the average Equivolume posting is about two increments wide, so instead of using 5- and 10-day moving averages, as we did in the time-based moving averages in our example, we will use 10-volume and 20-volume moving averages. That will give us approximately the same scaling. Please be sure to understand that we are averaging the last 10 entries, not the last 10 days. It will almost always actually be fewer days.

When we plot this information we see that the chart looks quite different (Figure 5.4). For one thing, the top on the price line is flatter because heavy volume traded there. That caused multiple entries and moved the plot sideways. This is, of course, an attribute of an Equivolume chart anyway—heavy volume leads to sideways plots. As in the prior chart of the simple moving averages (Figure 5.2), the next line to the right is the 10-entry moving average, and the plot farthest to the right is the 20-entry moving average. Note that they become progressively smoother as the number of entries used in the moving average calculation becomes greater, just as in the simple moving averages. Note, though, that the two moving averages both cross the price line, and cross one another, much earlier than in the simple moving average. We would see a more timely sell signal, no matter whether we were watching a crossover of the price with the moving averages or a cross-

**Figure 5.4 VOLUME ADJUSTED MOVING AVERAGES—
10-INTERVAL AND 20-INTERVAL**

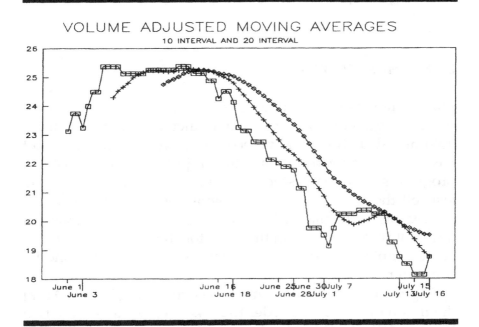

over of one another. In this case, at least, the volume adjusting is helpful in receiving an earlier signal. In addition, the signals are a bit less delayed on the small rally in early July. As a result, if one were trading the crossover of the 10-entry line with the price line, the whipsaw—while still not profitable—would be less harmful.

The reason that Volume Adjusted Moving Averages are often more helpful than simple moving averages is the fact that stocks or commodities tend to trade their heaviest volume at turning points. Volume is likely to be moderate during trends, but it usually expands dramatically on tops and bottoms. That means entries at tops and bottoms are likely to contribute more data points to the moving average, and therefore start to move the average sideways. The result is a tendency to bring in crossovers earlier, and therefore at more advantageous prices.

USING THE METHOD

This sounds like an awful lot of calculation and work. A simple moving average is not so bad to calculate and plot, but the volume calculations really become messy. Luckily we don't have to do it by hand, thanks to computer programs. With a program such as Metastock, it is all done very simply—you just tell the computer which moving averages you want to appear on your charts. You can even run it a number of different ways and put all the plots together on a single page. For example, let's look at another stock, this time done by computer.

Figure 5.5 is a chart of Cray Research during late 1994 and the first half of 1995. In order to make it easier to see the two Volume Adjusted Moving Average lines we have put them in their own box, above the Equivolume chart of the stock. In later studies we will not bother to do that; we will put them right on the price trace of the stock. That way the Equivolume chart can occupy more space and be more easily interpreted, rather than being crowded down to the bottom of the chart. That will be even more important when we also put the Ease of Movement oscillator on the page.

The two moving average lines are the 13-volume line and the 55-volume line. I have found these parameters to be quite effective, especially if one is trading the longer-term moves rather than the smaller swings. The smoother line, of course, is the 55-volume line.

In trading based upon the moving average lines one buys when the fast line (the 13 in this case) moves above the slower line (the 55 in this case). As can be seen, one would be short or

Figure 5.5 **CRAY RESEARCH—MOVING AVERAGE**

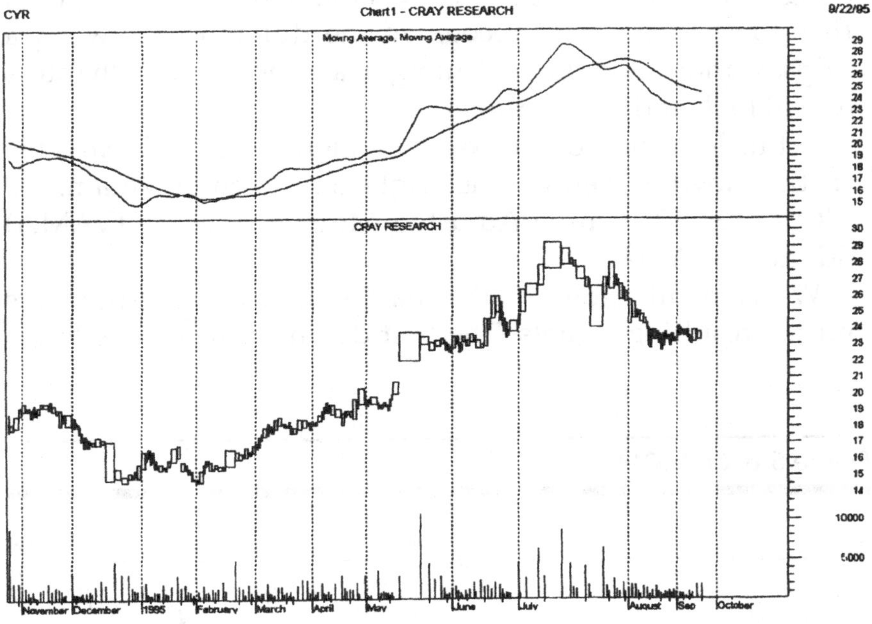

out of the stock at the left side of the chart. In the basing area
of the stock in January and February there are two small
crossovers, one producing a long position and the next a short
position; both would be unprofitable, but not disastrous. Then,
in February, we see a decisive cross to the plus side which
would suggest buying the stock. That would be a very profitable trade, with an upward move in the stock from about $16
to around $26 when a sell signal is given in late July. A short at
that time would also appear, as the stock chart ends, to be
working out well.

As with all moving average lines, we see that the profit
comes from a trending market. When the stock is moving
sideways in the base we suffer from whipsaws which bring
about losing trades. We are willing to swap a couple of small

losses for a substantial gain once the move begins. This is one of the reasons that moving averages are not, by themselves, enough of a methodology. They should be combined with other tools in order to recognize the difference between a whipsaw move and the beginning of a trend. In later chapters we will look at those methods.

Let us look at another example (Figure 5.6). This time we put the moving average lines right on the chart. Again, we will use the 13-Volume Adjusted Moving Average (VAMA) and the 55-VAMA.

We have put arrows on the chart to indicate the crossovers and the resulting signals. The first down arrow on the left is

Figure 5.6 **CITICORP**

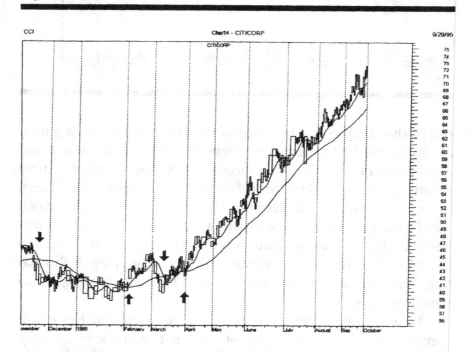

the start of a successful short position which is covered in early February. That is followed by a slightly successful buy and then a losing sell, before an extremely profitable buy in April. Again it is the sideways indecision in the stock which produces the small loss, and the long uptrend which produces the spectacular profit.

However, moving averages can be very effective in a sideways-moving stock if the swings are large enough. For example, in Figure 5.7 we see how Apple Computer cycled through three up and down waves in a period of less than a year. Using the 13- and 55-VAMA as before, we are able to make a number of profitable trades.

Prior to point A the long position would be a worthwhile one, as would the short from E to F, the buy at that point, and the final sale at G. However, some of the signals are too late to be profitable. The short at A would be a loss as would the next short at C. In addition, the very brief buy and sell from D to E would be costly. Overall, the swings allow a very good profit, even though the stock is in a sideways mode, because the swings are usually large enough. But it would be nice to fine-tune the system in order to maximize the profits. We have, to this point, arbitrarily used a pair of moving averages that appear to be quite helpful, but perhaps these are not the best parameters to be using.

OPTIMIZATION OF THE MOVING AVERAGE PARAMETERS

Let us stay with the same stock, Apple Computer, and see how we can improve trading results with the help of Volume Adjusted Moving Averages. Again, computer programs make this sort of study a good deal easier. It is possible, using our suggested programs, to test any number of variables in order to ascertain which parameters produce the best results. I

Figure 5.7 **APPLE COMPUTER—13-VAMA VS. 55-VAMA**

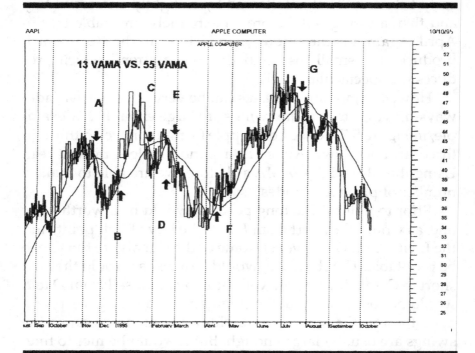

make the assumption that we want one of the two moving average lines to closely trace the actual price, but reduce it to a single line rather than a range of prices, in order to produce unequivocal signals. Therefore, I assign the value of three volume units to the fixed moving average line which will be tested against a wide range of other values for the slower line. In order to see which ones work best I ask the computer to test every second VAMA between 4 and 100.

The results we will look at are based upon four years of history in the stock. It is assumed that we are using $1,000 for each trade, and that we are not compounding the profits from trade to trade. Commissions have been ignored. Every crossover is acted upon, with no judgment as to its validity. And the results, in this stock, are quite spectacular.

As can be seen in Figure 5.8, the optimum moving average produced $4,467.62 in profits on the $1,000 over a four-year period. From there the profits declined, depending upon the value of the VAMA used. The last column to the right shows what moving average was used for each test. It should be noted that these are unusually strong results. Every moving average except the very smallest, the 4-volume increment, produced a profit. Most stocks tested would not produce such high numbers. But more important, all stocks produce profits at many VAMA levels, and the optimum values for the VAMA tend to be about the same in almost all stocks. That means that we can arrive at levels for VAMA that can be applied quite reliably to any stock we happen to be studying.

As can be seen in Figure 5.9, there is a peak in profits around the 20- to 24-VAMA levels. That would appear, at first glance, to be the moving average we should use in order to make profitable trades. There is another peak in profits around the 50-VAMA level, which comes close to the 55 we used in earlier examples. Then profits flatten out as we move out to longer values for the VAMA.

But there is another consideration. Some moving averages produce more trades than others. Looking at the table again, we see that the number of trades ranged from a high of 218 to a low of 20 over the four-year period. So, at the maximum, one would be making a round turn more than once a week, and at the other extreme, only a little more than one trade per quarter year. Let us look at the relationship of moving averages to trade count, since trades cost money in commissions.

Figure 5.10 shows that there is a very close relationship between the length of the moving average and the number of trades generated. The low VAMA levels produce a very high trade count, but then the line flattens around the 50-VAMA level. Obviously, the very high trade counts can be prohibitively expensive in terms of transaction costs. On the

Figure 5.8 APPLE COMPUTER, 4 YEARS—3-VAMA VS. 4–100-VAMA

Test number	Status	Net profit	Percent gain or loss	Total trades	Winning trades	Losing trades	Average win/ average loss	Option 1	Option 2
9	OK	4,467.62	446.8	58	28	30	2.37	3	20
10	OK	4,081.34	408.1	58	27	31	2.46	3	22
11	OK	3,368.13	336.8	54	25	29	2.28	3	24
8	OK	2,489.58	249.0	70	30	40	2.18	3	18
7	OK	2,108.05	210.8	76	30	46	2.29	3	16
4	OK	1,925.13	192.5	106	40	66	2.35	3	10
12	OK	1,669.18	166.9	54	24	30	2.03	3	26
6	OK	1,526.83	152.7	88	32	56	2.41	3	14
5	OK	1,523.62	152.4	98	35	63	2.51	3	12
23	OK	1,370.28	137.0	38	17	21	2.25	3	48
22	OK	1,227.85	122.8	32	15	17	1.98	3	46
21	OK	1,138.11	113.8	34	15	19	2.06	3	44
25	OK	1,092.69	109.3	32	15	17	1.77	3	52
24	OK	1,027.62	102.8	34	16	18	1.76	3	50
13	OK	1,019.96	102.0	50	21	29	1.98	3	28
3	OK	962.19	96.2	128	53	75	1.75	3	8
35	OK	853.10	85.3	22	8	14	2.62	3	72
28	OK	781.49	78.1	24	11	13	1.66	3	58
36	OK	750.15	75.0	20	8	12	2.12	3	74
39	OK	745.60	74.6	22	9	13	2.02	3	80
26	OK	739.50	74.0	26	12	14	1.57	3	54
41	OK	738.89	73.9	24	10	14	1.96	3	84
2	OK	730.24	73.0	160	60	100	1.90	3	6
14	OK	724.07	72.4	46	20	26	1.77	3	30
29	OK	700.89	70.1	24	10	14	1.87	3	60

Figure 5.8 (continued)

Test number	Status	Net profit	Percent gain or loss	Total trades	Winning trades	Losing trades	Average win/ average loss	Option 1	Option 2
34	OK	691.65	69.2	20	8	12	2.02	3	70
40	OK	662.80	66.3	24	10	14	1.88	3	82
38	OK	599.43	59.9	22	8	14	2.24	3	78
47	OK	575.23	57.5	21	6	15	3.42	3	96
20	OK	565.79	56.6	40	17	23	1.84	3	42
46	OK	560.26	56.0	23	7	16	3.04	3	94
49	OK	555.42	55.5	25	7	18	3.33	3	100
27	OK	547.08	54.7	24	11	13	1.47	3	56
48	OK	535.69	53.6	23	6	17	3.64	3	98
37	OK	531.38	53.1	22	8	14	2.12	3	76
45	OK	508.73	50.9	24	8	16	2.51	3	92
30	OK	508.70	50.9	22	9	13	1.73	3	62
15	OK	499.55	50.0	44	20	24	1.51	3	32
33	OK	483.19	48.3	24	10	14	1.66	3	68
42	OK	427.81	42.8	26	9	17	2.17	3	86
43	OK	427.81	42.8	26	9	17	2.17	3	88
32	OK	416.99	41.7	22	9	13	1.64	3	66
31	OK	398.17	39.8	22	9	13	1.62	3	64
44	OK	317.61	31.8	26	8	18	2.41	3	90
19	OK	316.59	31.7	42	16	26	1.91	3	40
18	OK	268.04	26.8	42	17	25	1.65	3	38
17	OK	253.66	25.4	44	18	26	1.61	3	36
16	OK	228.62	22.9	48	19	29	1.68	3	34
1	OK	−529.06	−52.9	218	77	141	1.41	3	4

Figure 5.9 **APPLE COMPUTER, 4 YEARS—**
3-VAMA VS. 4–100-VAMA PROFITS

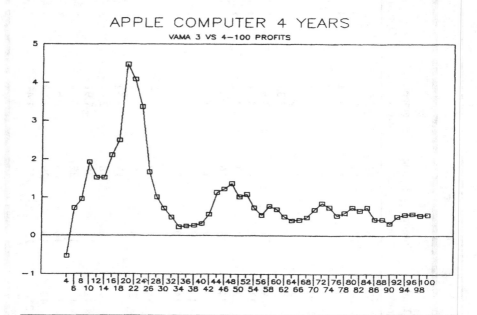

other hand, there seems to be little advantage in going out farther than the 50-VAMA region in order to try to avoid excessive transaction costs.

But let us see what this really means. Dividing the profits
at each level by the trade count at each level we come up with
a profit per trade at each level. We see a chart of the results in
Figure 5.11.

The peak is still there around the 20-VAMA level, but now
there is also a peak around 50 and another around 70. In addition, it is evident that the moving averages around the 35
level do comparatively poorly. These results are fairly typical
of the results obtained by doing similar studies on a great
number of stocks. Of course, they do not all produce such

Figure 5.10 **APPLE COMPUTER, 4 YEARS—**
3-VAMA VS. 4–100-VAMA TRADES

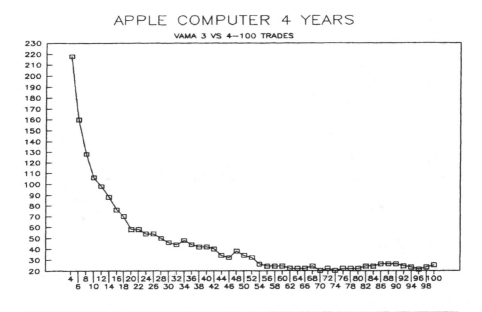

good results, and the optimum levels vary somewhat from stock to stock, but the results are similar enough for us to arrive at comfortable levels to use for our studies. For shorter-term, more aggressive traders I suggest using a 22-volume moving average, and for longer-term traders I suggest using a 55-volume moving average.

One might ask why we should make a distinction between two types of traders. Could we not just use the 22-VAMA and stick by it religiously? Why also look at the 55-VAMA? There are two reasons. One is that we are not going to be using Volume Adjusted Moving Averages as our single tool, nor as a strictly mechanical methodology. It will be a part of our over-all trading strategy, and a strong input, but will not be asked

Figure 5.11 **APPLE COMPUTER, 4 YEARS—3-VAMA VS. 4–100-VAMA PROFITS/TRADES**

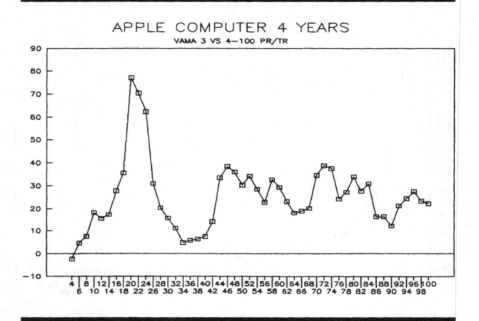

to stand alone. Consequently, the trading we do will still be a function of the way we read the charts. Sometimes we will be more interested in longer-term moves, and at other times we will be looking for short-term trades.

Second, all markets are not the same. Early in this chapter we observed that moving averages seem to be more effective in a trending market than in a sideways market. That is not always entirely true. A short-term moving average can help to catch the swings in a sideways market but take us out too soon in a trending market, whereas a long-term moving average can be very profitable in a trending market but produce whipsaws in a sideways market. We need to look at the optimum shorter-term moving average when we are trading a stock within a trading range, and then look at the optimum longer-term moving average when we are trading a stock which is in a trend.

Let us take one last look at the same stock, and see how the two different moving averages produce quite different signals. Figure 5.12 shows a small part of the history that produced the results cited previously. The upper window shows the 55-VAMA and its crossovers. It produces fewer trades and larger profits per trade. However, the signals are much later, and therefore a great deal of the move is sometimes missed. The center window shows the much more sensitive

Figure 5.12 **APPLE COMPUTER—3-VAMA VS. 55-VAMA AND 3-VAMA VS. 22-VAMA**

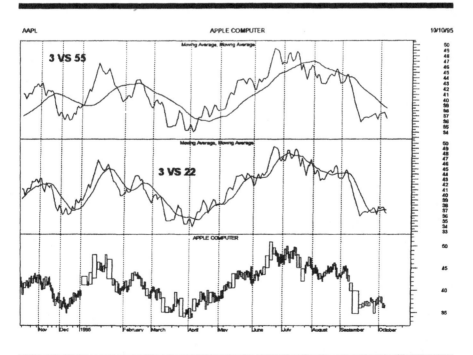

22-VAMA. Now many more trades are produced. The signals come in earlier, leaving less of the move on the table. On the other hand, there are more whipsaws and each profit is smaller. Neither of these is perfect, but each is helpful and will be very useful when combined with the other tools of the methodology.

Market Tides—Price and Volume Characteristics

TIDES, WAVES, AND RIPPLES

The concepts of tides, waves, and ripples go back at least to the writings of Charles Dow. He pointed out that there are major moves in the market which last many years. They are the trends, up and down, which continue for long periods of time and reflect the great underlying forces in the economy. They resemble the tides of the ocean.

Superimposed on the long rises and falls of the tide are the quite regular waves. They seem to beat in a repetitive rhythm and have a typical waveform. So, too, in the market, there is a regularity of waves superimposed on the tidal surges. As we will see in later chapters, those waves are sufficiently regular to be quite predictable, especially when measured on a volume basis. It is that predictability that will lead us to profits.

Finally, there are the ripples. They modify the shapes of the waves and are superimposed upon the waves. They are less regular and less predictable than the waves. Their pattern changes with every gust of wind. So, too, in stock trends—the ripples are less predictable and less regular, as every gust of fear or greed sweeps through the marketplace.

The great tidal surges on the ocean are caused by the very regular forces of the moon and sun, and are therefore extremely predictable. Unless a violent hurricane happens along, their height and timing is as regular as a metronome. Tide tables, which give the time, to the minute, when the tide can be expected to change direction, can be calculated for any location. So, too, the markets undergo long-term moves, which we call bull or bear markets. They are not as regular as the tide, but their long-term sweeps upward and downward are very predictable.

The forces that cause the oceanic tides are immense but distant. The tug of the sun and the moon draw the ocean up toward them, causing bulges that sweep around the globe. There is a lag time, however, so the bulge is not directly below the moon or sun, making the cause and effect relationship less immediately apparent. Primitive civilizations were aware of the regularity of the tides, but did not equate them with the heavenly bodies which cause them. It is important to note, however, that the observance of the tidal phenomenon was all that mattered. Knowing the cause did not help in predicting the rise and fall of the water.

So, too, with the tidal moves in the market. The causes are distant and not easily equated with the effects. Certainly the major upward and downward swings of bull and bear markets are a result of the underlying economy, but the relationship is distorted by the human emotions that lie in between. Anticipation brings in a lead time which is often so large as to cause markets to drop at a time when the economy appears to be booming, or to cause markets to soar just when the economic news is the worst. But, as in a primitive society, we do not need to know the forces that are creating the tides; we need only observe the swings from high water to low water and act in accordance with our observations.

The waves are caused by less gigantic forces than are the tides. Distant storms usually cause the waves. Therefore, they are a bit less regular than the tides and can vary more, depending upon the intensity of their cause. At one time the waves can be nothing more than a gentle lapping on the shore, only to be superseded within hours or days by huge crashing rollers. As with the tides, the cause of the waves is distant and therefore not immediately apparent. A typhoon off the coast of Japan can lead, much later, to great surfing in California. It is enough for the surfers to know that the surf is up and take advantage of it. The typhoon is the distant cause, but knowing about it is not necessary to profit from the conditions.

These same waves can be a menace to the unwary and unprepared. If unexpected or ignored they can send ships to the bottom. The usefulness and the danger associated with waves depends upon observation. One must look at the waves, not the typhoons that cause them.

The ripples are caused by local, and usually readily apparent, conditions. Every gust of wind can whip up a pattern of ridges. Within that short time frame they are quite regular, but a change of conditions can quickly alter their nature. These ripples are not usually large enough or long lasting enough to be of consequence. They can neither overturn boats nor transport surfers.

In the stock market our concern will be primarily with the waves. However, we cannot ignore the tides, and we should take advantage of the ripples. The ripples will be discussed in a later chapter; let us now look at the tidal moves in the market.

WHY STUDY THE TIDES IF WE ARE TRADING THE WAVES?

As I stand on the beach and watch the waves lap on the shore, I notice that there is a tendency for each succeeding wave to lap just a bit farther up the beach, wetting sand that had been dry. It may not be immediately apparent, since the waves are not all the same size, but if I spend some time studying the incoming waves I become aware of their tendency to move up the beach. I know then that it is a rising tide. There comes a time, however, when that advance seems to cease, and the waves no longer wet new sand but start to recede down the beach again. It is the turn of the tide. Now each succeeding wave will be a little lower than its predecessor.

In the stock market fewer waves make up the tide, so the tendency to have progressively higher tops and bottoms in a rising market is much more pronounced and noticeable. Similarly, the downward waves in a falling tide have significantly longer down legs and significantly shorter up legs. These facts make it important to know whether the market is rising or falling, even if we are only trading the waves within that market. The market direction gives a bias to the magnitude of the two sides of the waves. In an up market it is easier to make money by buying stocks than it is by shorting them. (By the way, if the idea of shorting a stock is new to you, don't worry about it. We will talk a good deal more about selling short in later chapters. Just understand that *shorting* is making money as prices go down.) In a down market it is easier to make money on short positions than on long positions.

We can see in Figure 6.1 how important this can be in a rising market. This is a steadily rising market during the bull move of 1964 and 1965. Shown on the chart are the tops and bottoms of each wave as the market advances. Because it is an advancing market the tops and bottoms are all higher than their predecessors. Note that the upward bias to the market causes each upward leg to be longer than each downward leg. Obviously, in this market there is more money to be made by buying at each dip and selling at each top than there would be if one sold short on each top and covered the shorts on each decline.

Figure 6.1 **DOW-JONES INDUSTRIAL AVERAGE 1956–1965**

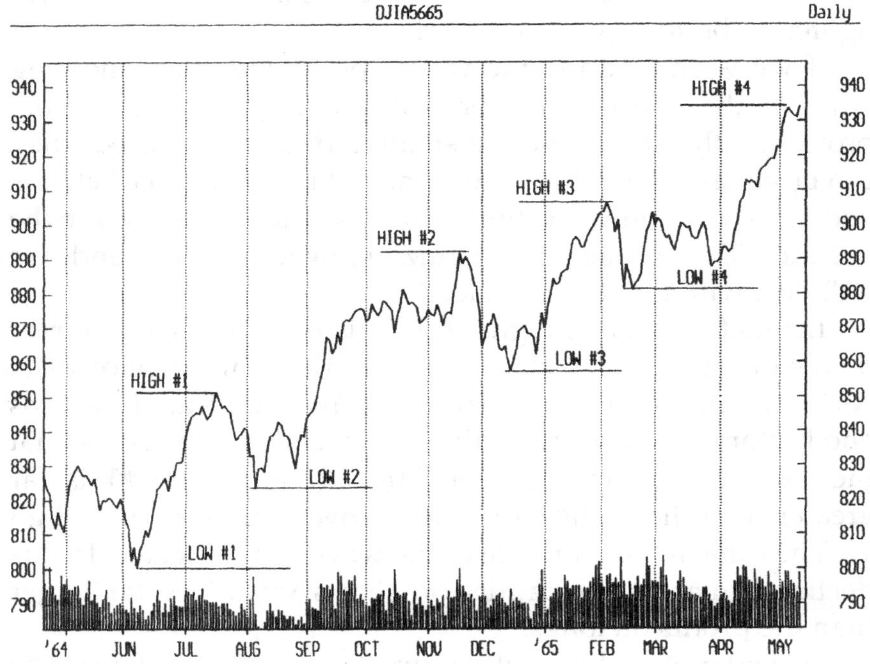

Notice another characteristic of these waves: Not only are the up legs more profitable, but they last longer. An up move tends to last about twice as long as a down move during an advancing market. The declines are sharp and brief.

Third, look at the volume trace across the bottom of the chart. Notice that the volume tends to be heavier on tops and lighter on bottoms. This is an important feature that will be even more evident when we go to Equivolume charts of the market.

From this chart, which is rather similar to any other rising market we might have chosen as an illustration, we have observed: (1) It is more profitable to be on the buy side in rising markets, (2) rising markets have legs that last longer in the up direction, and (3) volume tends to be heavier on tops and lighter on bottoms in rising markets.

If we wish to trade the waves profitably, then knowing whether the tide is rising or falling is important. Since the profits on the short side are small and quickly erased, they can be elusive. Therefore, if we know it is a rising market, it is better to trade only on the up moves and step aside for the declines. The problem is recognizing the long-term trend. We will deal with that further shortly.

Let us first look at Figure 6.2. This is very much a mirror image of the previous chart. It shows the bear move of 1977. As in the chart of a rising market, we have indicated the tops and bottoms of each succeeding wave. One can easily see that the vertical distance between High #1 and Low #1 is far greater than the vertical distance between Low #1 and High #2. The same is true for each of the waves on this chart. In this declining market the profits on shorts would be far larger than the profits on longs.

Second, notice the length of time involved in each leg. The downward legs are about twice as long lasting as the upward legs. The upward moves are quick and small, and therefore much more risky.

Third, let us look at the volume characteristics. Here we see that the volume is still—as it is in an upward market—heavier on the tops of the waves than on the bottoms.

So, based on this illustration, it appears that a trader of the waves will do better sticking with the short side in a declining market. Moreover, the down moves can be expected to last about twice as long as the up moves. However, it also becomes clear that the volume action does not change with the difference in direction of trend. Volume tends to be heavier on tops and lighter on bottoms, regardless of whether it is a bull or bear market.

Figure 6.2 **DOW-JONES INDUSTRIAL AVERAGE 1965–1977—DAILY**

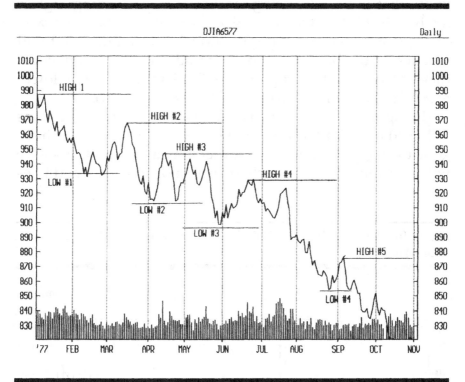

So, if we are going to trade the waves successfully, we must first be able to ascertain the position of the tide. Rowing against the tide can be very difficult, and we may find ourselves losing the battle.

PRICE MOVEMENTS AS A TIDE GAUGE

We are going to look at a number of factors which will help us to understand the market in which we are trading. The first of these is *price movement*, a subject we touched upon in the preceding section but which needs further examination. We know that in an advancing market each succeeding high is likely to be higher than its predecessor. That, in itself, is a way of knowing the direction of the tide. If we can draw a trend line across the bottoms, and the trend line has an up slope, then it is obviously an up market. Similarly, a series of lower tops tells us that it is a down market—a bear move.

In Figure 6.3 we see such an ascending pattern of bottoms followed by a similar series of descending tops. Here we have gone to an Equivolume chart rather than a bar chart, since we will be using Equivolume charts from now on and trend lines

Figure 6.3 **DOW-JONES INDUSTRIAL AVERAGE 1970–1977— MONTHLY**

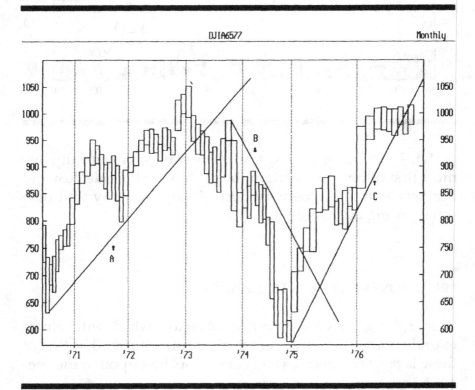

tend to be more reliable on Equivolume charts. Each rectangle represents one month of trading, just as each line represented one month of trading in the prior illustrations. Shown on this chart are the two segments—the up waves of a bull market followed by the down waves of a bear market—occurring between the market low of 1970 and the next market low in 1974. Notice that we draw a line across the bottoms on an ascending pattern and across the tops on a descending pattern. Often a secondary trend line, parallel to the first line, can be drawn across the tops of the waves in an advancing market (thereby defining a channel) and across the bottoms in a falling market, but they are usually not adhered to as strictly. Many times the up move will go out of the top of the channel in the later stages of the advance or down out of the bottom of the channel in the final stages of a decline. We see that happening in the bear move of 1973 to 1975. The decline accelerates in its final stage, violating the secondary trend line (the bottom line) as prices tumble.

The primary trend line also serves to tell us when a move has ended. Notice that the market penetrates line *A* in the down direction early in 1973, signaling an end to the bull market. Later in the year it returns to that line but is restricted from going any higher. Such a return to the old trend line is very common. We see the same tendency when we look at line *B*. It is penetrated by the up move in April 1975, but the next pullback, in October, comes down toward it, although not quite reaching it. Trend line *C* connects the bottoms of the next upward market. Notice that it is penetrated by the price at the last entry on this chart. Seeing this and knowing nothing about subsequent action, one would become concerned and surmise that the bull market was ending. (It was.)

As we observed earlier, the length of the up and down legs in each wave can be a strong indication of the type of market in effect. If up legs tend to last about twice as long as down legs in a bull market, then we should be able to tell fairly early in a new bull market that a change of direction has taken place by the duration of the up and down legs in the first few waves. Prior to the market bottom the down legs should be longer than the up legs, but after the market bottom the up legs should last longer than the down waves.

Figure 6.4 is a weekly based chart rather than a monthly based chart, allowing us to better see the component waves in a transition from a down market to an up market. We are looking at the bear market of 1920, in which the market lost half its value, followed by a bull market in 1921 and 1922. As can be seen in the first annotated wave, the horizontal dis-

Figure 6.4 **DOW-JONES INDUSTRIAL AVERAGE 1920–1922—WEEKLY**

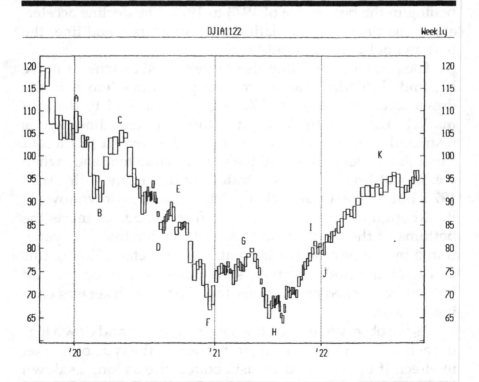

tance from *A* to *B* is longer than the horizontal distance *B* to *C*. That is to be expected in a declining market. The same is true of the next wave, where *C* to *D* is longer than *D* to *E*. It also holds true in wave *D-E-F*. However, the next wave—which is seen in retrospect to be the beginning of the formation of a turn to the upside—has quite equal legs. The distance from *F* to *G* is about the same as the distance from *G* to *H*. *H* is still lower than *F*, so that does not tell us that the decline is over, but the equality of the legs is a hint that a change may be taking place. The next wave leaves little doubt. The pullback is barely perceptible before the next wave starts. In addition, of course, the trend line has been decisively penetrated. But the early clue is the *F-G-H* wave with its similar legs. It hints of a change that could lead to the very strong waves *H-I-J* and *J-K-L*.

VOLUME AS A CLUE TO MARKET TREND

When we start to work with individual stocks in later chapters we will be very concerned with the fact that volume tends to signal price direction. Heavy upward volume is a sign of strength and is often a lead indicator of an imminent rise in the stock. The same is true in the overall market. In a sideways market, if volume tends to increase on advances and decrease on declines it is likely the next significant move will be in the up direction. Similarly, if volume tends to build up on pullbacks and slow down on rallies during a consolidation, the next significant move out of that consolidation is likely to be in the down direction.

Then, during the longer-term bull and bear moves, volume tends to be in the direction of the primary trend. When it is a bull market the heavy trading will be seen in the advancing segment of each wave, and the lighter volume will be seen in the declining segment. Figure 6.5 shows the

Figure 6.5 **DOW-JONES INDUSTRIAL AVERAGE 1944–1955—MONTHLY**

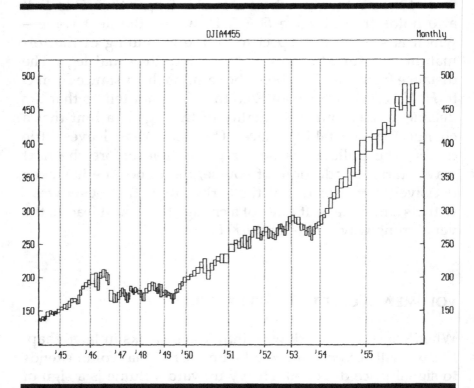

Dow-Jones industrials in the 12-year period from 1944 through 1955. First, let us look at the period from 1947 to 1950. This is a sideways consolidation. Because of the scale on this chart, the market setback in 1946, which precedes the consolidation, doesn't look particularly large. If we look more closely, though, we see that the market drops from over 210 to around 170, or almost 20 percent in a few months. That is enough to make investors apprehensive as to whether the consolidation is a precursor of another drop. However, looking at the monthly boxes that make up the consolidation we see that the up moves tend to be made on heavier volume and the declines on lighter volume. Here is a clue that the next move is likely to be a market advance.

There was another period of consolidation, from 1952 to 1954, which had the appearance of a top. After a long market advance that consolidation was sufficient to make most investors nervous, wondering if a big decline was in the offing. The pullbacks, however, were being made on light volume. There appeared to be no panic dumping of stocks. It looked as though the advance was not yet over, since volume still was concentrated on the up legs of each wave. As we can see, the advance resumed and volume expanded dramatically as the market shot upward for two years.

Compare that action to the consolidation at the top of the market in 1937, as shown in Figure 6.6. The market then also looked as though a top could be forming. The drop of February and March was made with heavy volume. A great deal of stock was being liquidated. However, volume had been heavy for a number of months anyway, so it was not easy to say that the decline was being made on heavy trading. But then the market rallied toward the old highs in July and August, and volume dried up significantly. The volume was saying that the rally lacked validity and that the market was turning over. The subsequent drop, which lasted into 1938, was a decline of more than 40 percent.

Another volume characteristic that is a clue to the position of the tide is comparative volume throughout the move. It is invariably true that volume tends to increase throughout a bull market, so that the heaviest volume comes in at or near the top. Unfortunately, that is most apparent in retrospect. In a bull market that has lasted for a long time we can observe that volume is becoming extremely heavy. However, it could still get heavier. Therefore, very heavy volume is a warning that an advancing market may be getting long in the tooth, but it cannot pinpoint the end of the advance for us. Later, looking back, we will be able to say, "Aha, the volume was heaviest as the top was being made!"—but that is after the fact.

Figure 6.6 **DOW-JONES INDUSTRIAL AVERAGE 1934–1943—MONTHLY**

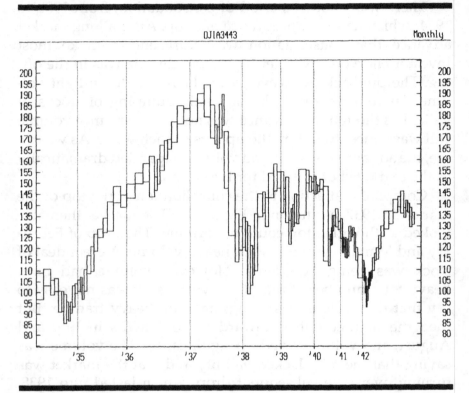

The previously mentioned tendency for volume to increase throughout the move applies, interestingly, only to upward moves. Volume does not tend to increase dramatically as a decline progresses. Often a bear market is terminated by very heavy climactic volume, but that is not usually preceded by a gradual building of volume. So, in a bear market, the volume over the entire move is likely to be fairly uniform, expanding only at the very last stage of the decline.

So far, we have looked at price movement and volume as two separate factors that tell us about the tidal moves in the market. However, Equivolume allows us to combine these two pieces of information into a single entry that imparts far more information. In the next chapter we see how that combination can be extremely helpful in ascertaining the position of the market.

Market Tides—Equivolume
and Ease of Movement

The often-used analogy to the market is a roller coaster. We picture the investor being swept upward and downward in smooth curving moves. Each rise ends abruptly as the speeding car swoops back downward, and each downward plunge ends with a breathtaking turn to the upside. The only force acting on the roller coaster once the wild ride begins is gravity, a downward force. Consequently, each upward move is more feeble than its predecessor, until the car finally comes to a halt at its lowest point. Often a bear market makes one think of riding a roller coaster, swooping ever lower on each wave. But the market is not driven only by gravity. There is the upward force of buying as well as the downward force of selling.

A better analogy might be a pogo stick. Here we have the upward force of the rider, legs pumping to accelerate each bounce, offsetting the downward force of gravity that forces the termination of each rise. The two forces always work against each other, causing an up and down sequence. Meanwhile, however, the rider moves forward. It takes energy on the part of the rider to make the pogo stick travel upward and forward; when that energy is expended the force of gravity pulls it back down to earth.

More important, look at the shapes of the paths traced by these two conveyances. The roller coaster's path has tops and bottoms that are both rounded—it looks like a series of sine waves. The path of a pogo stick has rounded tops and sharp vee bottoms. As we will see, the market's path tends to look much more like that of a pogo stick. The tops tend to last longer and be rounded, even on a bar chart, whereas the bottoms are more like a sharp downward arrow. On an Equivolume chart, as we shall see, this tendency is accentuated by the volume.

EQUIVOLUME CHARTING THE MARKET

So, let us picture the swings of the market as a ride on a pogo stick. If we really push hard as we leave the ground we will travel quite high and quite far, whereas a feeble push will give us only a short hop. By expending a great deal of energy we can even hop up a flight of stairs, each hop launching from a higher level than the last. With very little energy we can descend another flight of stairs. Our progress is a result of the amount of energy we are able to devote to the task.

Let us look at a typical pogo-stick market. In Figure 7.1 we see the bull and bear moves that made up the stock market action between 1915 and 1918. Certainly that was a long time ago, but this example could as easily have been selected from recent history. It is important to realize that market behavior is quite similar, regardless of the time period observed. Even though the market now trades almost a hundred times as high, in terms of the Dow, and volume has expanded even more, the way in which price and volume interact remains the same. Our examples are meant to show that the Equivolume principles are the same as they have always been. No governmental regulation, no amount of inflation, no revision of the

Figure 7.1 **DOW-JONES INDUSTRIAL AVERAGE 1915–1918—**
MONTHLY

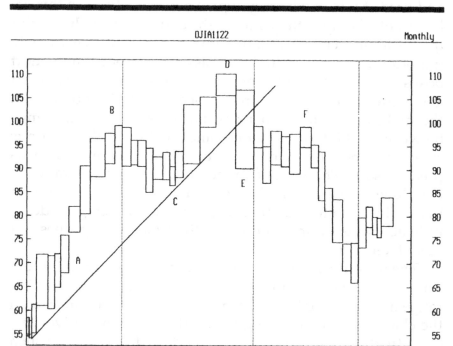

calculations can change the way human emotions force price
and volume to manifest themselves.

This is a monthly based chart. See how the tops at *B* and *D*
are rounded compared to the lows that precede them. In
terms of time there is quite a difference, in that one top was
made in about three months while the other was made in one
month. However, the single month *D* is so much heavier on
volume that it single-handedly produces the same sort of
rounding as the multiple-month lower-volume top at *B*.

Let us look at some other items on this chart, which show how Equivolume can help us to understand where we are, and predict where we are going, in a market. Prior to this we have looked only at the width of the entries—the volume. But the *height* of each box, as a function of its width, is extremely important. Tall boxes indicate easy movement while short boxes indicate difficult movement. We especially see short and wide boxes as tops are formed. At *B*, the volume on the highest month is not particularly heavy, but the range between the high of the month and the low of the month is small. The result is a rather square entry, compared to its predecessors. The lack of range suggests that the move is overdone. However, the lack of heavy volume is also a hint that a final top to the move is probably not being made. A pullback seems imminent, but a final market top does not seem likely yet.

The next top, at *D*, looks a lot more like an important top. The volume has expanded dramatically while the trading range has contracted, thereby producing a very square box on the chart. Anyone watching the market with an Equivolume chart (had one existed in 1916) would be startled to see such an entry and would be alerted to the fact that the market is obviously encountering resistance and is expending a great deal of energy trying to overcome that resistance. The top at *F* is also quite square, as the market attempts to move back up toward its old high. Again the squareness indicates resistance appearing, this time at a lower level. It is not as big a box, because it is not as important a top. It comes after the major top has been made and is part of the downward move that has taken over.

The shapes of the boxes between *A* and *B* are very informative. They are tall for their width, indicating easy movement in the upward direction. However, they still are wide enough to indicate heavy trading, lending credence to the move. Power is obviously coming in as the market moves higher. Just as short, fat boxes indicate resistance, tall, thin boxes indicate a lack of resistance. When a move is made with heavy volume and a wide trading range, it indicates the direction of power. Here we see that the power is in the upward direction. That observation is confirmed between B and C, where we see volume become lower and range also contract as the market backs off. The power is evidently not coming in on the downside. Between C and D the strength reappears. Volume expands significantly as the market again rallies, and the range also expands, producing wide but tall upward boxes. Power is still in the up direction.

Now let's look at the box at E, which is the month immediately after the very square top at D. An obvious change came over the market. Here, for the first time in a number of years, volume and range are expanding in the down direction instead of the up direction. This is a power box to the downside, and it very loudly announces that the market is in trouble. It contains more than a clue that the bull move is turning into a bear move. That is reinforced by the feeble rally to F, followed by further declines on substantial volume.

Another feature worth observing that shows up on this chart is the way in which gaps occur. Unlike individual stocks, gaps are rare in an average such as this. They are seen only when a very dramatic move hits the market. We do see a gap at the area marked A. Looking at the boxes on the two sides of the gap, we see that both are fairly tall and thin. That says that the market is encountering little resistance, and is running away to the upside. Such a runaway gap is a sign of strength and tells us that we are in a continuing upward move that probably has farther to go.

The next gap is very different. It is seen just before that very important box at D. It is a typical exhaustion gap, usually seen after a strong move. The box after the gap is much more square than the box just before the gap. It is another clue that a major market top is being made. Finally, we have a gap very near the end of the chart as the market appears to find support. In this case, it is more difficult to categorize the gap.

Coming after a long decline, it may be an exhaustion gap to the downside, in that the box after the gap is shorter than the box before the gap. However, the unimpressive volume makes it seem less likely that an important bottom is being made yet. We do expect a sharp vee bottom, as in the pogo-stick bounce; but we expect a more dramatic bottom, entailing both volume and price movement, if it is a major low being formed.

During long-term market moves we often see many inter-mediate-term tops and bottoms, each containing the features we have just observed but acting only as a part of the longer-term move. The 1916 high was dramatic enough to be quite convincing, but smaller boxes, which are nevertheless very square, can fool us into thinking a major top is being made when it is, in fact, only an intermediate-term hesitation. Such was the case in the market move that followed the breakout in 1982. With the market soaring into new high ground each month, there was an ongoing fear that it could end anytime.

Let us walk through the various boxes on that chart, Fig-ure 7.2, and see what they tell us about the direction of the market. The first important clue is the box marked *A*. After a series of months with little volume, price movement, or direc-tion, the entries can only be interpreted as a power box to the upside. The earlier highs around 950 are penetrated; volume and price spread expand. It is a period of market strength and alerts us to the fact that a change has come over the market. A sideways move has been superseded by an upward move. It is a very important month and emphatically demands that the Equivolume chartist pay attention. The next month is one of hesitation and consolidation. It is a very low range month, but without enough volume to suggest an important top. The market is absorbing the strength of the prior month. The month that follows, marked *B*, shows a resumption of the advance. It is another power box and says that the market appears to be embarking on an important move—that the breakout move was legitimate.

Figure 7.2 **DOW-JONES INDUSTRIAL AVERAGE 1982–1986—MONTHLY**

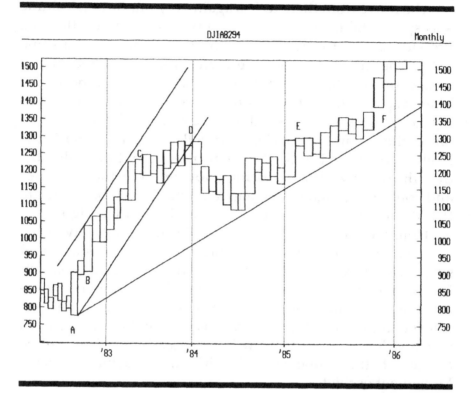

By the time the advance reaches *C* it has already gone a long way—a 50 percent advance off the low. Therefore, the series of square boxes there and at *D* warns that the market is getting tired and is encountering resistance. Remember, this is a monthly chart. The topping takes much of a year. The subsequent drop back lasts for six months and erases a good deal of the gain. However, volume does not increase significantly and there are no real power boxes to the downside. In addition, the tops at *C* and *D* are not made with dramatic volume, as we expect to see at the end of a bull market. Consequently, the evidence midway through 1984 suggests that it is only a pullback and that the bull move is likely to resume.

The move from there to E is again very important. Volume and spread both increase on the up moves, saying that the pressure is still to the upside. Box E is a more bothersome entry. The market reaches the high levels it touched over a year earlier—which happened to have been all-time highs. Then it spends the entire month in an extremely narrow trading range, finding it impossible to push through the old resistance; the squareness of the entry tells us that the market is likely to be turned back. It does turn back, but only slightly, over the next two months, before moving above the resistance and continuing higher. The gap at F and the tall box indicate that the market has regained power and is headed higher.

Here we have seen a few examples of how Equivolume methodology is used in market interpretation. The shape and size of each box have a story to tell as they reflect the conflicting forces of buying and selling. We see the times when movement is easy and the times when movement is difficult translated into boxes of varying shapes. That translation can take another form, as we saw in Chapter 4. Numbers can be assigned to the components of each box, producing an Ease of Movement oscillator.

EASE OF MOVEMENT

In looking at individual stocks, we decided that the 75 to 100 period Ease of Movement (EOM) gives the best results. We have to find different parameters to deal with the overall market. The reasons for this are the facts that the market shows a smoother progression than does the action of an individual stock, and that we tend to look at longer time periods when dealing with the market. It often seems as though the market is moving very rapidly, but looking back at the history of the market we see that the averages always move more slowly than most of their components. In a market that goes up 30 percent over a period of months—a very substantial move—some components will double, some will do very little, and a few will show a loss. This means that Ease of Movement studies must be more sensitive to compensate for the smoothing. For an individual stock, we will use a fairly long term EOM line in order to avoid whipsaws. With the overall market, whipsaws are less likely to be a problem. Moves are smoother, so reversals are more reliable.

When trading individual stocks, we try to work within the trend of the market. We want to trade the long side in bull markets and the short side in bear markets. That means we need to be cognizant of the longer-term trend of the market— a trend that is larger than the swings we wish to trade in the individual issues. For this reason we tend to look at longer-term charts of the market; we often use weekly or even monthly charts and look at many months or years of trading history.

Computer-testing a great number of possible Ease of Movement parameters, we came up with some interesting results. We looked at the last few years of history and started with weekly posted Equivolume charts. Not surprisingly, the very low Ease of Movement numbers produced large profits, but at the expense of a great number of trades. Going out a bit farther, we found that the 15, 16, and 17 EOM parameters produced good profits on a reasonable number of trades, bringing the profit per trade up to an acceptable level.

For example, the 15 EOM produced 10 long positions in an 8-year period, as shown in Figure 7.3. There are a few whipsaws, but the signals kept the trader long in all the important moves and helped to avoid a number of setbacks. These signals are long-term enough to be used as a guideline in assessing the overall market. However, the market was in a period of long-term advance. Just being in the market throughout the period would have been very profitable. Looking further, we

Figure 7.3 **EASE OF MOVEMENT—LONG-TERM DOW**

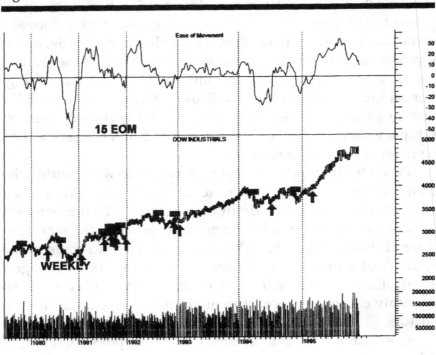

find another area of EOM values which also behaves well. That is the level around 50 to 55. There are far fewer trades than in the 15 area, thereby raising the profit per trade. It is a very long term indicator, most valuable in long-term trending markets. A part of that chart is shown in Figure 7.4.

The three-year period from mid-1992 to October 1995 is shown. It is the second half of the previous chart (Figure 7.3). As can be seen, the 55 parameter produces a far less volatile EOM line. The chart says that it is a bull market, until January of 1994, when the EOM drops below the zero line. Throughout much of 1994, when the market is flat, the EOM is saying that there is more pressure on the *sell* side than on the

Figure 7.4 **EASE OF MOVEMENT—WEEKLY DOW**

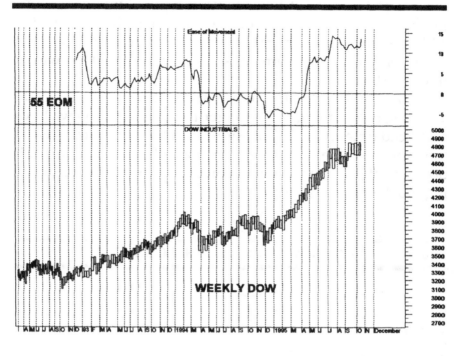

buy side. That changes in early 1995, after the bull market resumes. The 55 is quite a bit later than the 15, but it avoids many less significant market fluctuations.

However, perhaps using weekly charts is still too sensitive. Ideally, we would like to know only what the broad tidal sweep of the market is doing. From 1982 until the time of this writing (in late 1995), the market has been a major bull market. The advance has been punctuated by only two significant drops, and even they were only part of the long uptrend. The first setback was the panic of October 1987; the second was the Gulf War decline of 1990. Otherwise, the best policy was to be on the long side of the market. To find the optimum

EOM level, we gave the computer the entire bull market to look at and applied it to a monthly Equivolume chart. Surprisingly, the number again came out to be a little above the 50 level—the same general area we found to be effective on the weekly charts. Figure 7.5 shows how a 58 EOM would have worked.

It does tell us to stay in a market, which is in a steady advance, but in going to the longer-term information we have sacrificed timeliness. The *sell* signal in 1987 is too late to avoid the drop, as is the *sell* signal in the Gulf War decline. In addition, it waits too long to signal you back into the market, missing much of the advance.

Figure 7.5 **EASE OF MOVEMENT—MONTHLY DOW**

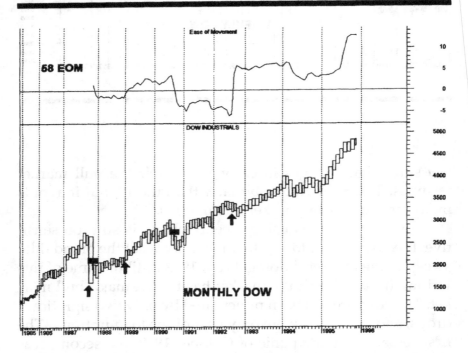

It appears that the best use for Ease of Movement in working with the overall market is to apply it to weekly charts. I like to look at both the 15 and 55 EOM as guidelines. The 15 will give an earlier signal, but one that may soon be negated. The 55 EOM is later, but tends to define the longer-term trends. A crossover of the 15 EOM is a signal that should not be ignored. We saw such a crossover in early October 1987, before the huge drop. Similarly, the 15 EOM kept the trader out of the Gulf War decline and gave a timely signal to come back in. Watch the 15 to see the immediate signal, and then watch the 55 as well to confirm that the signal is not being negated. If the 55 does not soon follow the 20 in a crossover, I begin to question the validity of the signal.

In this chapter we looked at the application of the Equivolume principles, both through direct chart reading and Ease of Movement numerical analysis. These techniques form the foundation for knowing where we want to be in the market. In the following chapter we go to Volume Adjusted Moving Averages as another confirmation and look at the cyclicality of the market as a further clue of what to expect in the future. All these tools should be used in conjunction with one another. We are, however, following a logical progression from technique to technique. In Chapter 6 we saw the long-term trends in the market and the characteristics of major bull and bear markets. Then, in this chapter, we considered the individual postings and their relationships to each other. We went farther by applying Ease of Movement. Notice that we have gone from the larger picture to the smaller picture. This is the way our thinking should progress as we work in the market: from the largest market moves to the smaller considerations. In the next chapter we narrow our view even further as we look at the Volume Adjusted Moving Averages and consider the various cycles which operate in the market. That will eventually lead us to an even narrower view when we consider individual stocks in later chapters.

Market Tides—
VAMA and Cycles

Volume Adjusted Moving Averages (VAMA) provide additional valuable indicators of the probable future direction of the market. As with our work on individual stocks, however, results vary greatly depending upon the parameters used. In searching through a large number of possibilities we find, as we did with the Ease of Movement (EOM) work, that two general levels produce good results in a consistent manner. One is shorter term and contains a number of small, losing trades in order to participate in the longer-term moves. The larger moving averages avoid the small mistakes but are less timely. They swap whipsaws for timeliness.

WATCHING THE VAMA

As with the EOMs discussed in the preceding chapter, I find that I want to watch both levels. The more sensitive takes precedence over the longer term, but the longer term must soon confirm the short-term signals or I become apprehensive about the validity of the crossover. Of course, as with individual stocks, the greatest strength of moving averages is the recognition of trends in trending markets. In sideways markets whipsaws are almost unavoidable when relying upon moving averages. We can see this in Figure 8.1—the moving average is extremely effective in the two major upward legs, but it gives a number of signals which accomplish little during the sideways move seen near the center of the chart.

However, this chart shows the results of using the optimum shorter-term Volume Adjusted Moving Averages. The very short term 3-VAMA is meant to define the price trend, reducing it to a single line but not deviating far from it. The 24-VAMA is less sensitive. In studying many alternatives, we found a bunching of good results, without generating an inordinate number of signals, around the 24 level. Therefore, we

Figure 8.1 3-VAMA VS. 24-VAMA—WEEKLY DOW

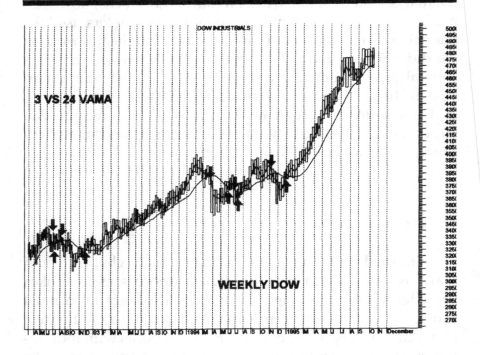

will use that level as the most important VAMA indicator when looking at weekly market charts. The up and down arrows on this chart designate the points where the two moving averages cross one another, generating *buy* and *sell* signals. Notice, at the far left of the chart, that the second up arrow is very timely in getting us into the market. From there the two moving averages remain in the up mode for about 16 months, a period when the Dow goes from 3,200 to 3,800. That move more than compensates for the two earlier signals, which were of little profit. Similarly, the last up arrow at the start of 1995, which is still in effect at the chart's end, more than makes up for the two earlier signals in 1994, which may have been slightly profitable but did not produce major moves.

The chart covers a period of about four years; the market was in a longer-term advance, but with two sideways consolidations. In attempting to eliminate the whipsaws, we went to the longer-term VAMA that had been found to produce optimum results: That is the 100-volume level, as shown in Figure 8.2.

As can be seen, however, the 1994 sideways consolidation was enough to produce a couple of useless signals even at this level. In addition, the 1990 to 1991 drop during the Gulf War gave a *sell* signal and then a *buy* signal, which were both so late as to cause a loss. The longer-term index did continue to suggest, with its constant upward slope, that the bull market was still in effect. But it did so at the expense of erroneous and late signals. Consequently, in looking at the weekly charts, I prefer to use the 24-VAMA to tell me where I should be in the market and watch the 100-VAMA for a more general idea of the long-term market.

I also like to take an even longer-term outlook into consideration. Figure 8.3 shows a monthly rather than weekly chart, which allows us to look at about ten years of history without losing detail.

The two moving average lines are again volume adjusted and are again based upon tests of many possibilities to ascer-

Figure 8.2 3-VAMA VS. 100-VAMA—WEEKLY DOW

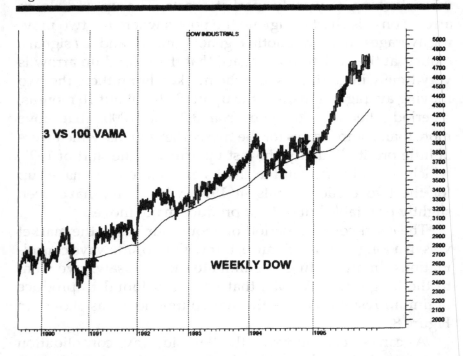

tain the optimum parameters. The more sensitive line, which closely tracks the price, is again the 3-VAMA. The less sensitive line is the 10-VAMA. Interestingly, little has been gained in effectiveness over the prior work on the weekly charts. The consolidation areas in 1990 and 1994 still produce whipsaws, and the longer upward trends still produce big profits. In addition, we now see the 1987 panic. The signal here is too late to avoid the debacle. The value of the monthly chart is primarily in its ability to give a longer-term view of the market. The two moving average lines confirm the trends we have already identified on the 24-VAMA weekly chart, but they tend to be late. I follow the monthly chart primarily to maintain a perspective on the long-term market trend, rather

Figure 8.3 **3-VAMA VS. 10-VAMA—MONTHLY DOW**

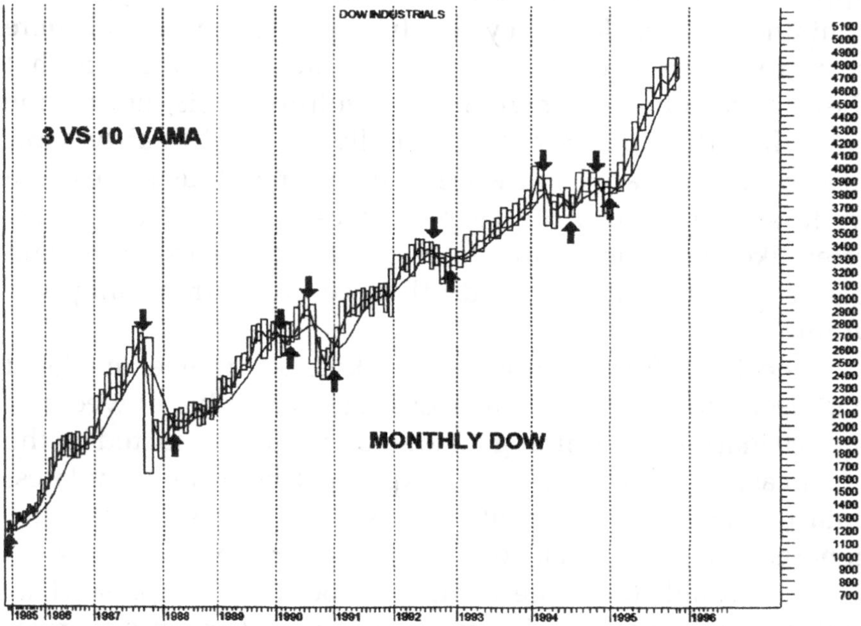

than as an aid in making a decision. The moving averages tell whether the trader is in a trending market or a consolidation market, but they are too slow to give action signals.

CYCLES

As we saw in Chapter 3, there are cycles in individual stocks which appear to be based upon a volume frame of reference rather than a time frame of reference. We see that tops and bottoms tend to occur in a very regular rhythm—a volume rhythm. This was actually first noticed when working with the overall market rather than individual stocks. Shortly after developing Equivolume charting, I became aware that there appear to be cycles in the market and that those cycles are contained within larger cycles. In the other direction, there seem to be smaller cycles, also. The interesting thing is that they seem to be very regular on a volume basis, not a time basis. In individual stocks we usually work with fairly short histories, so we are less aware of the tremendous increase in trading volume over the years. In looking at the market we often like to go back many years in order to try to profit from past experience. When we do that we notice the changes in volume.

I recall my first months as a stockbroker trainee, in 1961. I had been sent to the New York office for a number of weeks of indoctrination and training. One session was conducted by the head cashier of the firm, who explained how the very latest data processing equipment was used to process trades and generate confirmations. To educate our group of trainees, he led us through the huge computer room and impressed us with the company's ability to process very large numbers of orders. He ended the tour by telling us that the modern equipment would have no trouble keeping up even if the market were to consistently trade six million shares every day.

Today we consistently see trading days in excess of 400 million shares on the New York Stock Exchange alone. That does not even include NASDAQ, which often exceeds the NYSE in volume. The increase in volume over the years has been a very constant progression.

This increase in volume brought the concept of volume cycles to my attention and eventually led to its incorporation into the Equivolume technique. I saw that the regular tops and bottoms on weekly and monthly market charts tended to be nearly equidistant on an Equivolume chart. However, the cycles were very different if I looked at a time-based bar chart instead of a volume-based Equivolume chart. As volume in the market became heavier, the time between tops shrank. On the Equivolume chart they looked equidistant, while on a time-based chart the cyclicality was lost as the cycles became shorter and shorter.

In *Volume Cycles in the Stock Market,* published in 1988, I illustrated a number of the cycles in the market and identified a very important and consistent cycle that could be traced back for many years. It appeared that the market made a low every 16 billion shares. That, in turn, appeared to be punctuated by a cycle half its size at 8 billion shares. In addition, there was a much smaller cycle of about 700 million shares recognizable on the daily charts. Today, with trading so much heavier, 700 million shares are likely to be traded in less than two days. Any cycle of that short a duration disappears completely.

At the time of that book, the duration of the 8- and 16-billion-share cycles could be measured in months, whereas a few years previously they had taken years to form. Today, we need to look at a daily chart and use a little imagination to discern those cycles. Instead of many months, the 8-billion-share cycle now lasts a little over a month, and will probably be even shorter in years to come.

The smiling faces on the chart in Figure 8.4 designate the lows in that cycle. Note that they are very nearly equidistant on the horizontal axis. They are a little over a month apart. During the time pictured, the market was trading about 6 billion shares per month, so these bottoms are being seen about every 8 billion shares. This is the cycle that used to last years! The frowning faces are the intermediate tops between each pair of lows.

It seems that the 8- and 16-billion-share cycles have lost much of their usefulness. It is worthwhile to watch them as a clue to short-term market swings, but they are not very helpful to answer the more important question: Are we in a bull or bear market? They are now only minor punctuations within the larger market swings.

Let us look again at a long-term picture of the market. Within the great upward move from 1982 to 1995 there were a

Figure 8.4 **CYCLES—DAILY DOW**

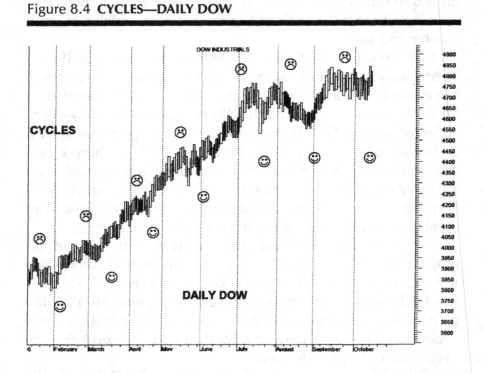

number of corrections of sufficient magnitude to be important. We had the pullback to the breakout level in 1984, the
panic in 1987, the Gulf War in 1990, a significant pullback in
the second half of 1992, and the sideways consolidation in
1994. On Figure 8.5, each of these lows is indicated with a
smiley face. They are nearly the same distance apart. However, if we look at the time frame, we see that the increasing
market volume is still shortening the time frame. The first two
smiley faces are about three years apart; then it takes less than
three years to the next one. The cycle after that takes about
two years, as does the last one on the chart. Here we seem to
have a cycle that we need to watch. It appears that the market
becomes overbought and ready for a rest on a regular basis,

Figure 8.5 **CYCLES BY EQUIVOLUME—WEEKLY DOW**

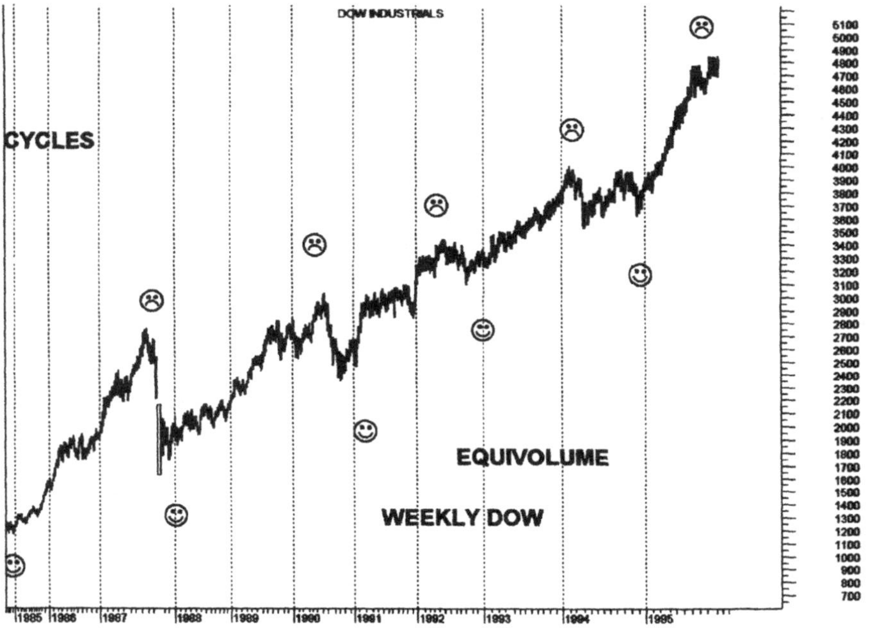

based upon the number of shares that have been traded. That cycle has a duration of about 120 billion shares. This does not mean that we should add up the shares traded, and bail out of the market at exactly that point in the volume. It does mean, however, that we should watch our charts closely, and anticipate a correction before long. If you have replaced three sets of tires on your car after you have used them for 40,000 miles, then it makes sense to check your spare tire when you have 39,000 miles on the next set.

Knowing Your Market

When we started this discussion of the market we observed the fact that the market consists of tidal movements modified by wave patterns, and those wave patterns are further disturbed by ripples. So far, we have looked primarily at the long tidal moves in the market, and have tried to ascertain what sort of major market we are dealing with. Let us now put all of these factors together and see what type of market we are dealing with.

At any given time the longer-term market can be doing one of four things: (1) It can be trending up, (2) it can be trending down, (3) it can be doing nothing after an advance, and (4) it can be doing nothing after a decline. We primarily tend to think of markets as having only two possible directions: up or down. However, as we can see looking back over history, the market spends a good deal of time moving laterally. The strictures "know your market" and "the trend is your friend" condition us to think that the market is always either a bull or bear market. In reality, the market tends to spend far more than half its time (and volume) in consolidations.

It moves rapidly from consolidation level to consolidation level, then languishes in that area for quite some time before another spurt. A consolidation can be a reversal area, where a bull market becomes a bear market or vice versa, or it can be a resting area prior to a resumption of the trend. Figure 9.1

Figure 9.1 DURATION OF MARKET PHASES

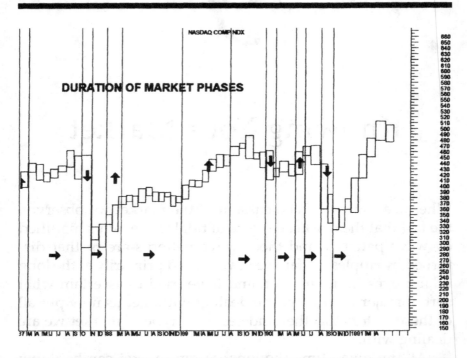

shows the comparative time spent in consolidation areas and in trending phases of the market. Up and down arrows indicate trending phases, while the horizontal arrows indicate consolidation phases. As can be seen, a great deal more time is spent in consolidations than in trends.

After a market has had a big advance, the tendency is to look for a top. A sideways move after a rise usually brings in the predictions that a top is forming—that the bull market is over. In reality, a move is at least twice as likely to continue as it is to reverse. Looking back over many markets of the last century, we see that, for every time a market reverses its direction after a consolidation, there are two times when the trend resumes after the consolidation. This means that trying to call a market reversal rather than assuming the trend will continue is a dangerous occupation. The odds are two to one that we will be wrong.

This does not mean, as we shall see, that one should not look for market reversals and try to capitalize on them. It does mean, though, that one must be aware of a great deal of other information beside the fact that the market has "gone too far, and looks ready to reverse." Figure 9.2 shows a series of bull and bear moves in the Dow transportation index. The consolidations are labeled as either reversals or continuations. Notice that there are far more consolidations that lead to a continuation of the trend than consolidations that turn out to be reversals of the trend.

Figure 9.2 **CONTINUATION OR REVERSAL**

CHARACTERISTICS OF BULL MARKETS

Recognizing the direction of a trending market is a good deal easier than recognizing the eventual direction of a sideways consolidation. This is especially true, of course, after it has been in the trend for some time. By then, though, a large part of the opportunity presented by that observation may be lost—it has become late in the game. So, the sooner a new market trend is recognized, the better.

Figure 9.3 shows the indications one should watch for to identify a bull market. They do not all become immediately obvious, and some may not always appear, but they are the earmarks which can tell the trader that a bull market is in progress.

The most reliable indication, and the first factor one should search for, is the location of volume. Even early in a new bull market the volume will expand on up moves and contract on declines. After forming a base, a move out of that base on heavy volume—especially with a widening spread—announces a change of direction.

Looking back at Figure 9.2, for instance, we see that the first upward move from the lows, at the center of the chart, is

---

Figure 9.3 **CHARACTERISTICS OF BULL MARKETS**

Volume increases on up waves.
Volume decreases on down waves.
Volume increases as move progresses.
Lows are higher.
Highs are higher.
Up legs last longer than down legs.
Cycle bottoms are equidistant.
Ease of Movement is positive.
Moving averages are positive.
Boxes are tall and narrow.
Market moves off a good base.

made with heavier volume. As it hits the first consolidation of the move, we see that it has gone through the prior resistance with much heavier volume. That suggests that a new bull move is under way.

In the prior decline, volume came in on down moves and dried up on rallies. Now we are suddenly seeing a different sort of market. Volume is now going to the buy side. In addition, of course, the descending trend has been reversed. The base is so narrow at the low that it seems unlikely that the rally can go very far without some more base building, but the upward move has certainly given a strong signal that the bear market has become a bull market.

The first pullback has heavier volume than one might anticipate, but the decline does not go very far before a new up leg with heavy volume and a widening price spread gets underway. From then on, each rally is made with heavy volume and each decline is made with lighter volume. Later in the move we also see that volume has increased over the life of the move. That, too, is typical of a bull market, but it is not evident until much later in the move.

Evident only a little later than the volume characteristics is the pattern of higher highs and higher lows. By the time we see the second rally, it is obvious that an uptrending pattern is forming. Since volume is heavier on the upside than the downside, the pattern of short declines and longer advances also becomes evident early in the move. Even if the same number of time periods constitutes the two sides of the waves, the heavier volume on the up legs make them longer lasting on a volume basis, as money flows to the buy side of the market. While perhaps not a distinct characteristic, the regularity of the cycles is part of the previous observations. The lows tend to be equidistant as the market advances. In a down market, the more reliable cycle measurement is top to top, while in a bull market, the lows tend to be equidistant, and the highs tend to wander more. Actually, the tops tend to move farther to the right as the bull market becomes older, while the lows remain quite regular.

The shape of the Equivolume boxes is also a good clue. Taller boxes are usually seen on the upside and shorter boxes on the downside, if it is a bull market. This, combined with the fact that volume tends to increase on up moves, means that an advancing market consists of a series of power boxes in the direction of the major trend. They are usually seen as the averages penetrate successively higher resistance levels, adding evidence of a strong underlying tone to the market. As a bull market progresses, I like to look for those power boxes. They tell me that the market is still healthy.

A lasting bull market is generated by a strong base. A very narrow bottom, without much testing and base building, is unlikely to lead to a substantial and lasting market move. There must be a reason for the move, and that reason is a period of accumulation. Before a large market move the wisest of investors usually accumulate a great deal of stock. The more stock they accumulate, the more likely they are to hold that stock for a major move. Consequently, wide bases (in terms of volume) tend to lead to more profitable market rises. A move out of a very narrow base worries me, since it appears to be unsustainable.

As a bull market begins, we should see Ease of Movement go to the plus side, and the Volume Adjusted Moving Averages should cross in the plus direction. Typically, these signals will be seen early in the move. In Figure 9.4 we see the move off the market low in late 1988 and early 1989. After the panic drop in 1987 the market goes through a long period of base building. There is formidable resistance around the 2,200 level in the Dow, which repeatedly turns the market back. After the 1987 drop, investors are extremely skittish, looking for another decline. By mid-1988 the two moving average lines cross to the plus side, however, reflecting the upward bias in the base and suggesting that an advancing phase, a bull move, is starting.

Figure 9.4 **EOM AND VAMA, 1988–1989**

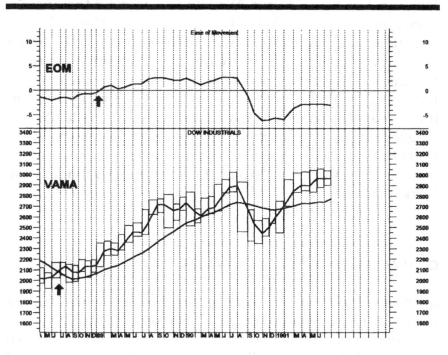

Interestingly, this signal is seen long before the Ease of Movement crosses to the plus side. That does not happen until early in 1989. By then the very encouraging monthly posting of February is occurring. The early warning comes with the VAMA crossover. That is reinforced by the increasing volume and widening of the spread in February which shows that the market is emerging from the base. The presence of a bull market is confirmed at the same time by the crossover of the EOM line. The result is a strong market advance, taking the Dow to almost 3,000 before the setback which accompanies the Gulf War. The width of the base prior to the breakout is a clue that it will be a substantial move.

Finally, a bull market is likely to start in an area where a long-term cycle low is due. We saw in Chapter 8 that there is a tendency for the market to form long-term cycles with lows and highs quite equidistant. The cycle does not tell the trader to become a buyer, but a move out of a consolidation area is more believable if the cycle work says that an up cycle is due. If the market starts upward at a time when, on a cycle basis, the market low should be made, it suggests that a legitimate longer-term move is starting. It is part of the evidence which leads to the conclusion that "We are now in a bull market." I need to reach that conclusion before becoming a longer-term market buyer.

CHARACTERISTICS OF BEAR MARKETS

In most respects we can reverse our thinking when dealing with bear markets rather than bull markets (Figure 9.5).

The Equivolume boxes will be taller and wider on down moves, and the rallies will usually have higher volume and smaller ranges. We will see a series of lower highs and lower

Figure 9.5 **CHARACTERISTICS OF BEAR MARKETS**

Volume decreases on up waves.
Volume increases on down waves.
Volume increases as move progresses.
Lows are lower.
Highs are lower.
Down legs last longer than up legs.
Cycle tops are equidistant.
Ease of Movement is negative.
Moving averages are negative.
Boxes are tall and narrow.
Market moves off a good top.

lows, which produces a down channel. In addition, we will see that the down part of each cycle will be longer than the up part of the cycle. We saw that in bull markets the cycle tops tend to be skewed to the right, while the lows remain equidistant. In bear markets the regularity of the cycles is better observed in the tops, while the lows tend to be skewed progressively farther to the right as the bear market progresses.

Near the start of a bear market we will see the Volume Adjusted Moving Averages cross in the negative direction, and we will see Ease of Movement move to the minus side. This should come quite near the beginning of the bear market, and it is likely to coincide with a power box to the downside. As in the start of a bull market, the power box is probably the most important indication. It causes a penetration of support and usually also penetrates the ascending trend line. These are the early indicators I look for to be convinced that a bear move has started.

Later in the bear market the other characteristics become more apparent. The down legs of each cycle will be seen to contain more volume than the up cycles, and the pattern of lower highs and lower lows will show up.

As in a bull market, the fact that it is a trending market rather than a consolidation market is evidenced by the taller and narrower boxes. These boxes will tend to be in the direction of the primary trend—in this case, downward. Rallies will be on lighter volume, but also on shorter boxes.

CHARACTERISTICS OF MARKET TOPS

As we have observed, consolidations can be reversals or they can be resting phases in a continuing move. Recognizing the difference between the two can be extremely important. In addition, we know that continuation moves are about twice as common as reversals. It is natural to look for a top after a big market advance. There is a fear of a rapid reversal that could take away all those pleasant profits. In reality, however, if we know nothing else and we assume that there is no way to differentiate between consolidations, the odds are still two to one that the move will continue rather than reverse. The fact that the market has been in a strong upward move, which we are likely to see as a negative, is, in fact, a positive. For some reason—and probably not for any readily apparent reason—demand is the stronger emotion and prices are rising. A consolidation does not indicate that the situation has become bearish, but only that a status quo has been reached. Buyers and sellers are in equilibrium, and therefore prices are moving sideways. Until further evidence comes in, the assumption must be that the underlying forces that pushed prices higher are still there and that the next move is likely to be a continuation of the trend. Therefore, when we look at market consolidations and try to define a top, we must remain aware that we are looking for the more unusual move.

In future chapters, as we look at individual stocks, we will have a different attitude toward consolidations and be less anxious to try to second guess the direction of the move after the consolidation. But evaluating the market is a somewhat different story. Here, a market break—a major market top—can be very costly, very rapidly. In addition, market consolidations usually last longer than the consolidations of the issues which make up the market averages. Sitting through a consolidation can mean having money at risk and doing nothing for a long period of time. Recognizing a probable reversal and going to the sidelines greatly reduces risk, and if the move later turns out to be a continuation rather than a reversal, there is time to go back in. So, let us look at market tops and identify factors that give us clues that they are truly tops, with a drop imminent (Figure 9.6).

Figure 9.6 **CHARACTERISTICS OF MARKET TOPS AFTER BULL MARKET**

Heaviest volume in move is seen.
Boxes are square.
No downward bias is evident.
No decrease in volume is evident.
Tall box is followed by a square box.
VAMA is negative or whipsaws.
EOM is going negative.
Power box to the downside is seen.

Perhaps the best clue that we are witnessing a market top rather than an intermediate consolidation is seen in the volume. First, volume will be the heaviest seen at any time since the market advance began. Second, volume tends to decrease in a continuation-type consolidation; in a reversal-type consolidation volume tends to stay heavy and become even heavier as we move across the consolidation. Therefore, I always watch the trading as a market moves sideways after an advance to see if volume tends to dry up or continues to be heavy. This tendency shows up fairly early in the consolidation, so positions can be exited and money can be taken off the table well in advance of a breakdown.

In conjunction with continued heavy trading, it is typical for the market to move laterally, or even move slightly higher, during a consolidation; however, if the move is eventually to resume, the consolidation is likely to have a downward bias. In an intermediate consolidation, it is as though the market absorbs some selling, then backs off under the selling pressure and gradually dissipates it, as evidenced by the decreasing volume. Conversely, in a final top the buying pressure remains heavy and pushes the market upward against resistance with no decrease in volume, until the bears suddenly gain control and prices drop precipitously.

On an Equivolume chart the shape of the boxes can be very informative. In a final top we tend to see many square boxes continuing across the top. Usually, they are more square than the postings that made up the prior market rise, and they are usually butting up against an obvious resistance level. The first box in the consolidation is likely to be quite square and will often come right after a tall box, in that a powerful upward move has suddenly encountered resistance. From there on, the boxes tend to continue to be square, especially any time the old high is approached. This is quite different from a typical intermediate consolidation, where the first box is less likely to be so square, and subsequent boxes tend to be smaller, with a downward bias.

It does not become evident for some time, but a final top is likely to last a good deal longer, in terms of both time and volume. With the heavy volume, this becomes even more apparent on an Equivolume chart. When I see a consolidation that has moved a long distance laterally, I become more concerned that a major top may be forming. The market is continuing to have extreme difficulty in overcoming a formidable resistance level. Of course, as the lateral move continues a number of other indications come into play. For one thing, if a market that has been in a strong advance moves sideways for very long, it will eventually penetrate the ascending trend line—saying that the up move has ended. That does not, in itself, dictate that the next move will be down, but it certainly says there is a strong possibility that it will be.

Another effect of a protracted consolidation, especially one with continuing heavy volume, is a convergence of the two Volume Adjusted Moving Averages, so that any weakness brings about a rapid crossover. There may, in fact, be a number of minor crossovers in both directions as the lateral move continues. Whipsaw action of the moving averages, therefore, becomes in itself a signal that the consolidation has lasted too long, and warns that a change of trend is likely. Almost the same thing can be said for Ease of Movement. In an intermediate consolidation it usually does not have time to cross over to the sell side, but the heavy volume, the lack of range, and the overall duration of a final top is likely to push the Ease of Movement toward—or even to—a crossover while the consolidation is still in progress.

Of course, the final evidence that the consolidation is a top, not just a resting phase in a continuing advance, is the power box to the downside that takes the market out of the consolidation. By then it should have been quite evident from the previous considerations, but the power box is hard to miss. Increasing volume with a widening spread through the old support produces a tall but wide box on the Equivolume chart, stating unequivocally that the sellers have taken control.

Looking back over the bull market tops we have seen this century, we find that the preceding observations hold true quite reliably in every top. Figure 9.7 shows how each of these markets has made its final top. In every case the heaviest volume of the entire move comes in as the market starts to top.

Figure 9.7 **MARKET TOPS IN HISTORY**

Year	Heaviest volume	Sideways	Volume steady	Squares	Power box
1912	Yes	Yes	Yes	Yes	Yes
1916	Yes	Yes	Yes	Yes	Yes
1919	Yes	Yes	Yes	Early	Yes
1929	Yes	Yes	Yes	Early	Yes
1937	Yes	Yes	Yes	Yes	Yes
1966	Yes	Yes	Yes	Yes	Yes
1972	Yes	Early	Yes	Early	Late
1977	Yes	Yes	Yes	Yes	No
1987	Yes	No	Yes	No	Yes

That is followed by a sideways to somewhat higher formation with volume remaining very high. In 1972 there was an exception. The sideways move began earlier, but was then followed by another upthrust into new high ground. As a consequence, the squares also squared early on the Equivolume chart, creating a move that is sometimes seen in individual stocks but is not common in the entire market—an upthrust after distribution. The top was forming with very heavy volume and a narrowing spread, creating square postings, but a final buying surge came in, which may have sucked in the last buyers before the collapse. A further result of this unusual activity was a postponement of the power box to the downside. It came in later, as the market dropped through the bottom of the earlier sideways formation. In 1919 and 1929 the squares also came a bit early, followed by a final upthrust that could not hold.

I have included 1987 in this listing. It was not, however, a typical top, and should probably be considered only as an intermediate correction within the very long bull market that began in 1982. It did not build a sideways area and never had the square postings we have come to expect. The power box was actually a collapse that took the market all the way to the bottom of its move. It looked then, and still looks in retrospect, like a sudden panic—only a punctuation within a long-term advance.

CHARACTERISTICS OF MARKET BOTTOMS

A market bottom is not the mirror image of a market top. Recalling the analogy of a pogo stick, we note that bounces at the lows are very different from the rolling over of the tops. They do have attributes, however, which often make it very obvious that a major low is developing. They usually do not look at all like the consolidations on the way down, making the job of differentiating them a bit easier.

The most striking evidence of an important low is the presence of *panic*. After a market has worked its way lower for some time, there comes a point when investors become really scared and dump stock indiscriminately. In the process, a number of things happen. The trend downward becomes much steeper, penetrating the bottom of the channel that has been defining the down trend. Volume becomes very heavy as stocks are randomly dumped in large amounts. Price swings in both directions become very large as emotions overcome all logic. Such action is very different from the typical consolidation on the way down, in which volume is likely to become lighter during the countertrend move. On the final washout, volume remains very heavy and there is less likely to be a well-defined countertrend move. Market lows are made in the midst of an emotionally charged atmosphere, with most investors convinced that prices will go much lower. Only a very cool and unemotional trader is able to step in and buy under such conditions.

The second part of the bottom formation is the *test of the lows*. It may be a few days, a few weeks, or even months later that the market takes another look at the low point reached during the original washout. In 1962, it was months until the Cuban missile crisis caused a test of the low. The second low—the test—can be higher, the same as, or lower than the original low. That is not as important as the fact that *volume should be lighter on the test*. In 1974 the test came two months after the original drop, and the market actually went a little lower, but volume did not increase on the penetration of the old low—in fact, it decreased. That was strong evidence that the market was making an important bottom.

As with a top, the final confirmation comes from a power box—this time in the up direction. It is very likely to penetrate the down trend defined by the recent rally highs, and it will take the market through the highest point reached between the original low and the test low. The result is a formation that looks like a *W* on the chart. But the first bottom of the *W* will be on much heavier volume than the second, and the breakout will be made with a power box.

Of course, opposite the formation of a top, the Ease of Movement starts to move in the positive direction, and the two moving average lines cross to the plus side as the new upward move begins. They are likely to be a little less timely than on a top, because of the abruptness of some bottom formations.

In Figure 9.8, we see how the major market lows of this century conformed to the various signals. In all cases except 1942 (and, marginally, 1915), the heaviest volume in the market move was seen as the climax low was being made. In 1942, that may be a result of quiet trading during the war. In every case, the market low was followed by an identifiable test of the low. In no case did the market simply make a single low and then progress upward. Also, in each case the volume on the test was lower than it had been on the original climax.

Only in 1932 did we not see the wide price swings and panic trading that are usually associated with a low. It was as though the market had seen so much panic selling after the

Figure 9.8 MARKET BOTTOMS IN HISTORY

Year	Heaviest volume	Climax and test	Wide swings	Power box
1915	?	Yes	Yes	Yes
1918	Yes	Yes	Yes	Yes
1921	Yes	Yes	Yes	No
1932	Yes	Yes	No	Yes
1942	No	Yes	Yes	Yes
1962	Yes	Yes	Yes	Yes
1974	Yes	Yes	Yes	Yes

1929 top, and had gone so low, that it was by then exhausted. It did have a volume low and lighter volume test, but it was a less emotional turn than usually seen. The power box to the upside was evident in every case but one: 1921. In that case, it was a gradual move upward after the other normal requirements of a market bottom had been met.

Long-Term Arms Index

The Arms Index was originally created as a tool for intraday trading—to help one know how to time trades during a single trading session. Later it became apparent that a moving average, such as a 10-day moving average of the index, could be very helpful in ascertaining the short to intermediate swings in the market. Soon Wall Street traders were using it primarily in that way. A few traders then started to look at it in a broader way, with a 21-day moving average, in order to see the intermediate-term market swings. Here, too, it was found to be effective. It appeared that the index, originally designed as a short-term trading tool (and even originally named the Short Term Trading Index), had applications to longer-term markets that went way beyond the needs of the trader.

In this chapter we complete our study of the broader swings in the market by looking at how the Arms Index can play a part in our decision-making process. We will see that the Arms Index is effective even in ascertaining the very long-term position of the market.

CHARTING THE EXTREMES

As with any use of the Arms Index, we want to look for extremes. The index tends to move from overbought to oversold positions, regardless of what time frame we are looking at. That is, the index produces bullish numbers for so long that it becomes overbought, having been too bullish too long. Then, as bearish numbers are produced, it eventually becomes oversold because too many bearish numbers come in for too long. Also, remember that the index numbers tend to move contrary to prices, so bullish numbers are low numbers and bearish numbers are high numbers. People often find this confusing. It seems more logical that big numbers are good and small numbers are bad, whereas Arms Index numbers work in just the opposite manner. I tell them to think of it as a golf score, where low numbers are desirable and high numbers are undesirable.

This results in peaks on the market that tend to coincide with the troughs on the Arms Index. Whether we are looking at a 5-day moving average and trying to trade the ripples or looking at a 200-day moving average to see where the tide is, we will always look for times when the AI is at an extreme high as a sign of a market low and look for an extreme low in the AI as a sign that the market is at a high. On the two charts of the index and the market average, posted one above the other, the two lines act as though they were attached to each another by an elastic cord. They move far apart only to be pulled back together. Let us look at such a pair of charts, in Figures 10.1 and 10.2.

We are looking at a very long period in history, a 15-year time span starting in 1969. The first chart (Figure 10.1) depicts the 100-day moving average of the Arms Index over those years, while the second chart shows the Standard & Poors 500 stock index over the same period. The two highest points in Figure 10.1 can be seen to coincide very well with the low points of the market. Here the elastic cord effect is quite apparent. It is as though the two lines stretched apart and were then pulled back together. Following on across the

Figure 10.1 **100-DAY ARMS INDEX—1969–1984**

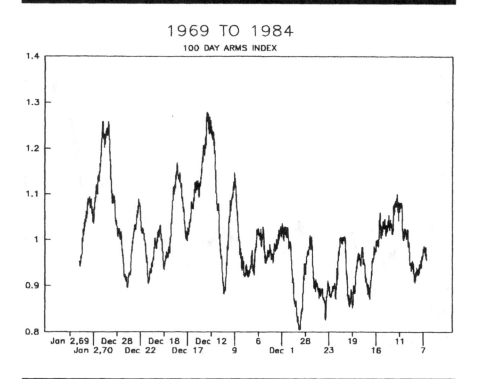

chart, the same action can be seen repeatedly—low points on the market correspond to high points on the index, and vice versa. As the market drops lower, big Arms Index daily numbers are generated. Long periods with many big numbers reflect a preponderance of selling, a bearishness which eventually becomes overdone. The moving average moves to very high numbers, indicating that the selling has gone on for too long and a reversal in the market is due. That is the type of indication we see on the two major peaks in this chart.

Figure 10.2 **STANDARD & POORS 500—1969–1984**

1969 TO 1984

S&P 500

ACCURACY, SENSITIVITY, AND TIMELINESS

Looking for overbought conditions, we must look at places where the 100-day AI nears the bottom of its chart. Again, we see a number of times when the AI becomes quite low, and they coincide well with high points in the market. However, these points are not as pronounced, or as similar in level, as the *buy* signals were. It appears that a smoother line, a longer-term moving average, might be desirable. However, in using moving averages of prices, even Volume Adjusted Moving Averages, we found that a longer-term moving average, by its very nature, makes signals come in later, thereby missing the best price levels. Each time we move out to a longer moving average, we trade timeliness for accuracy. A sensitive moving average is more timely but is prone to whipsaws and false signals. It would seem logical to assume that a longer-term moving average of the Arms Index would similarly lose its timeliness as it is smoothed.

Amazingly, that is not the case. Because we are dealing with a moving average of an index, not an average of prices, the effect is very different. A longer-term moving average does, as we would expect, smooth the line, making it less equivocal, but it does not appreciably move the peaks and troughs to the right. In Figure 10.3, I have calculated 200-day

Figure 10.3 **300-DAY, 200-DAY, AND 100-DAY ARMS INDEX—1969–1984**

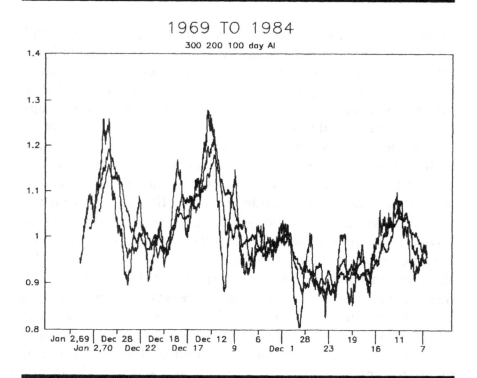

1969 TO 1984

300 200 100 day AI

and 300-day moving averages of the AI for the time period shown previously, and superimposed that prior chart.

Notice particularly the two major peaks in the index that we saw as such good *buy* signals before. The most volatile line, of course, is the 100 day-line we looked at before. The line below it, which does not go quite as high and has fewer gyrations, is the 200-day line. Below that, and smoother still, is the 300-day line. These peaks are very nearly directly below one another. Almost no timeliness has been sacrificed in smoothing the lines. Therefore, it would seem that we could use a fairly long term moving average to remove the false signals, yet not arrive late at the party.

CLOSE-UP ON SMOOTHING

In Figure 10.4 we have isolated the 300-day line to see if it will give better signals. Referring to Figure 10.2 as a market indicator, we see that the market lows, indicated by the peaks in the AI, are still very good. In fact, the smoothing has made the lower peak near the end of the chart much more obvious, suggesting a buy point just before the rapid advance in the market that terminates this chart. This 300-day line also does far better in recognizing overbought markets. Toward the left side of the AI chart, between the two major peaks, is a low area in the index which, while not dramatic, suggests that the market is becoming overbought. Later, when the AI makes its lowest postings on the chart, it tells us that the market has become very overbought. That area was so confused on the 100-day chart as to be hard to interpret. On the 300-day chart, though, it becomes an overbought zone, warning the trader to be cautious. However, one should not lose track of the fact that these are very long term charts. Even areas that look like sharp reversals last a number of months. This index is not meant to pinpoint turns, but rather to serve as an indicator of

Figure 10.4 **300-DAY ARMS INDEX—1969–1984**

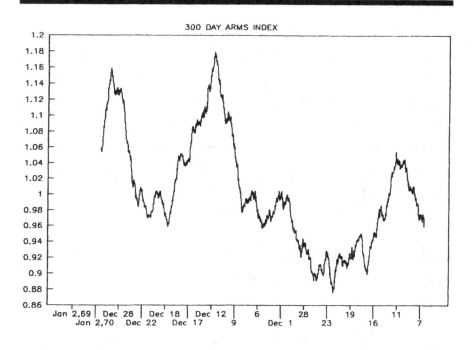

300 DAY ARMS INDEX

the overall condition of the market. But extremes in this index can be very useful—for example, its behavior in 1987, just prior to the October panic (Figures 10.5 and 10.6).

In Figure 10.5 we see two very low points on the Arms Index, punctuated by a sharp high point between them. The first low came in just prior to the market break in 1987. It reached the very overbought condition in the 300-day line shortly before the market break began. Anyone watching this long-term indicator would have been forewarned of the impending collapse.

Then, after the market had lost about 30 percent in just a few days, the AI went to a spike on our chart. With the public terrified, the index said that, even on a 300-day moving aver-

Figure 10.5 **300-DAY ARMS INDEX—1983–1995**

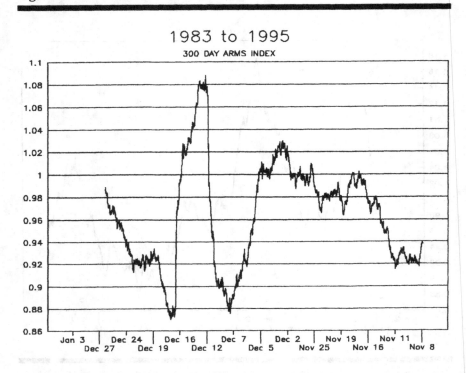

age basis, the market was extremely oversold. It suggested buying, in spite of the fear permeating Wall Street.

The next signal was the second major low point in the index. It came after a substantial market advance and, more important, prior to the Gulf War bearish move. Another good call.

After the Gulf War, the 300-day moving average of the Arms Index worked its way higher—not as high as the prior peak, but high enough to warn that a new bull move could be starting. After that, until the end of the chart, the index moved toward the overbought area, and the market moved continually higher. Again, the index high foretold a good opportunity to buy stocks for a profit.

Figure 10.6 **STANDARD & POORS 500—1983–1995**

I always keep an eye on the longer-term position of the Arms Index. It is certainly not a way to pinpoint buys and sells, but taken in conjunction with all the other tools we have explored in the last few chapters, it can be a powerful confirming indicator.

A Stock to Buy

We have spent the last six chapters looking at markets from many different angles to learn how to ascertain the type of market we are dealing with at a given time. Moreover, with the help of cycles, volume studies, the Arms Index, and Ease of Movement we are able to tell, in a general manner, where we are within a particular part of the cycle—whether we are in the early, middle, or late stages of a bull or bear market. That can be very important in helping us decide which stocks to buy. Although there are classic chart formations that can be said to usually lead to profits, different patterns are more reliable and more profitable in different market stages.

A smart investor should try to ascertain the stage of the market and match trading to that phase. Not only are stocks going to be bought on a different basis at different times in the market, but the level of exposure and the time frame for investments will vary, depending upon the market phase. In the middle phases of a bull market, one wants to be fully invested and hold situations for long-term gains, if possible. In a sideways market, one may need to be satisfied with shorter-term moves and smaller gains. In what appears to be a market top, one would like to limit risk by being only partially invested.

THE FIRST RALLY OFF A BEAR MARKET LOW

Let us start at the end of a bear market. It is perhaps the most dramatic action we ever see in the market, and is therefore the most easily recognized. We saw in the previous chapters that a bear market termination is usually characterized by a very heavy volume washout, which takes the averages down so sharply as to penetrate the bottom of the descending channel. This action is also reflected in similar climactic action in many of the individual stocks.

As a bear market ends, there is usually complete capitulation—all of the stocks have been knocked down, the good ones and the bad ones. Quality is of no consequence as everything is sold indiscriminately. The stocks that will be the best buys are likely to act as the market is acting—finding support after a washout and rallying impressively from the low. This is a market for quick capital gains. The stocks have not yet had the opportunity to build wide bases, so we cannot expect long-lasting moves. Any buy at this time is a speculative position, not a longer-term investment.

Perhaps there is no more difficult time to be a buyer than on a climax low. The market is in the grip of rampant fear. It is difficult to retain objectivity and recognize this fear in others without succumbing to it yourself.

The fear usually comes after a long period of demoralizing erosion of prices, when the decline is capped off by a sudden violent downward plunge. Volume becomes very heavy as everyone seems to be running for the exits at the same time. At this time the press will make dire forecasts, as will many respected market commentators. This is, however, one of the times when one must be a contrarian, not a trend follower. It should be apparent to the technician that the emotion of fear has become extreme and unreasoning.

Remember that the market consideration is the determining factor when becoming a buyer at this stage. Later on in a bull market the individual stocks will be more important than the market in determining actions, but a climactic market is a highly emotional market wherein the individual issues are likely to be moving together.

In late 1990, the market had been down for a number of months as the war in the Persian Gulf intensified. In mid-October the final washout low was made (see Figure 11.1), followed by a quick reversal—both moves with heavy volume. The decline had moved the averages down out of the bottom of the descending trend, suggesting a very oversold condition. The cycle was also due to make a low in the vicinity, and the Arms Index had become quite oversold, on both a long-

Figure 11.1 **DOW-JONES INDUSTRIAL AVERAGE—WEEKLY**

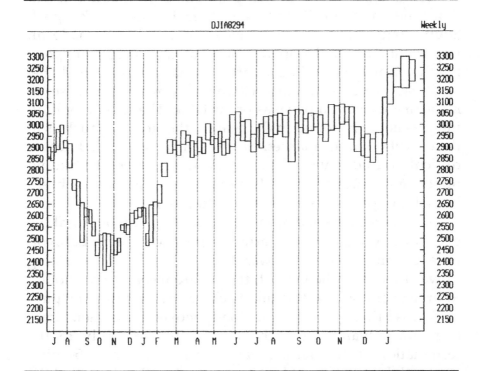

term and short-term basis. A rally could be expected, but the narrow base could probably not support a lasting move without some further consolidation and base building. After a climactic low, a secondary test on lighter volume was also to be expected. It looked like a time to buy a few stocks for a speculative move. It was not, however, a time to become fully invested on a longer-term basis. All we could really know at that time was that the market appeared ready for a rally. It was not likely to last very long, and could be only a resting point before going lower. An opportunity for a successful trade seemed to present itself, but only for an aggressive and flexible trader. In retrospect, it was an important turn that led to a continuation of the longer-term bull market. A sharp drop in early 1991 was made on light volume, thus confirming the turn in the market and widening the base.

Let us look at a stock that provided a profitable trade at that time. In Figure 11.2 we see a weekly chart of Campbell Soup Company. In the first week of October it made an important move in the up direction, coming off a square posting the prior week and penetrating the descending trend line. This was a sign of strength. There was, however, no base, so no lasting upward move was predictable. The reason for buying was not to be found in the chart of the stock as much as in the condition of the market. After a sharp market decline it is difficult to find any stocks with substantial bases, so trading opportunities must be found among stocks with narrow bases but with impressive signs of strength.

After some consolidation the stock did go higher until the end of the year, when it started to produce square Equivolume postings. Since we were not convinced of a lasting upward move in the market, the square weeks were enough to urge profit taking. Looking back, we can see that the pullback was brief. The stock eventually moved far higher. However, the advance from the top of the first rally to the termination of the first leg was over 4 points on a 25-dollar stock. We had no way of knowing, based on the chart, that the

Figure 11.2 **CAMPBELL SOUP COMPANY—WEEKLY**

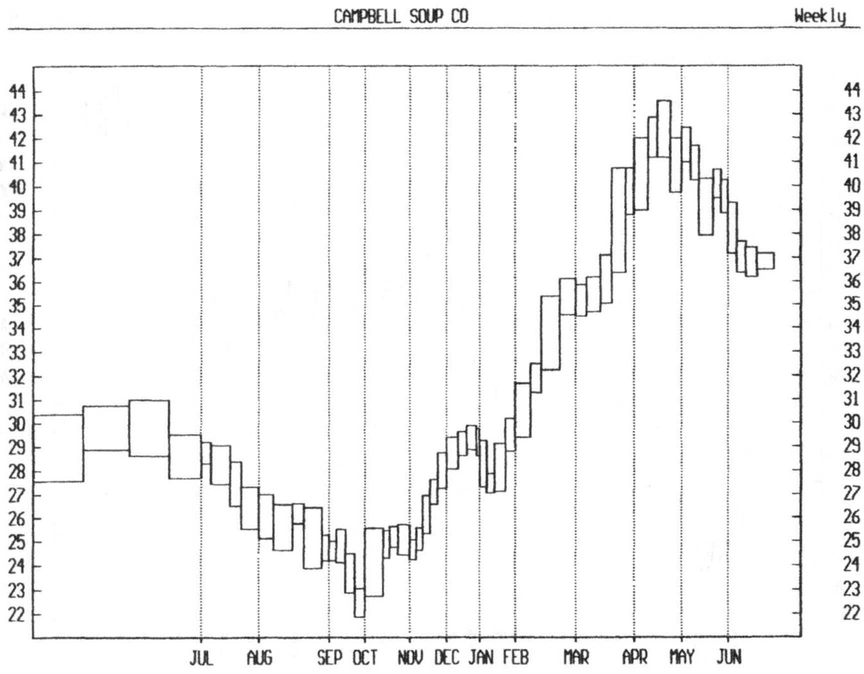

CAMPBELL SOUP CO   Weekly

move would eventually take the stock over 40. Only later did the stock generate another *buy* signal.

Before moving on, let's look at another stock coming off a climax low. In Figure 11.3, we see Eaton Corporation as it trades off the same market climactic action in 1990.

Note that there is no climactic action in this stock, but only a squaring at the bottom which indicates it was meeting support. However, it had been in almost a free fall prior to that squaring, which took it out of the bottom of the descending channel. A buy in November of 1990 could be justified only on the basis of the market, with the square entry suggesting

Figure 11.3 EATON CORPORATION—WEEKLY

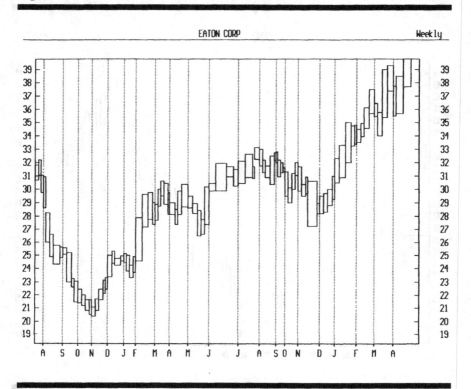

this stock was ready to move higher. The rally to 25 before the next pullback is risky but profitable. The square entries in the 25 area are a signal to take a short-term profit.

The next opportunity to be buying stocks is seen after the market makes a successful test of the prior climactic low. As we know, the test is expected to be made on lower volume and is not necessarily at the same level as the original low. It is usually not as low a point, but there are instances when the test is below the original climax. The real indications of a successful test are lighter volume, a squaring of the entries, and a rally that breaks the descending trend line of the pullback.

Stocks bought at this time are considered to be a short-term position since the old rally high may restrict the move. When the buy is made, it is made with the anticipation of a small gain in a fairly short time period. However, since the market has given a strong indication that it has made a valid longer-term turn, there is a strong probability that the rally highs will be pierced. Consequently, positions should not be closed out too quickly if the stock moves, as anticipated, back to the prior rally high. It is likely to make a volume breakout at that point, taking most stocks with it. In Figures 11.2 and 11.3 that is exactly what happens. In early February the market suddenly rockets through the January high, making the six months which have gone before look like a wide base and the launching pad for a substantial advance. Both these stocks go upward through the old resistance with heavy volume and a widening price range—an impressive sign of strength. The move from the pullback low to the resistance would be quite good, but the eventual moves as they participate in the resumed bull market are far larger.

When we find ourselves at a point that appears to be a pullback low as a test of a prior climax, some money should be committed, but it is not the time to become fully invested. There is still a strong possibility that the market will move sideways rather than turn upward. In doing those buys we look for support in the individual issue, with some squaring of the entry. That support is likely to be at the top of the old consolidation which was seen on the first low. For example, the Campbell Soup Company in Figure 11.2 comes down to the 27 area and then produces a square box on this weekly chart. The top of the consolidation in October was around 26, so the stock is acting quite strong. From there, volume increases as it goes back up to the resistance and eventually penetrates it. The anticipated profit is the advance from 27 to 30, but the lack of much hesitation in the 30 area, and our realization that there is a potential for a breakout in the market and in this stock, is a reason to hold the stock and wait. The breakout in February is the start of a magnificent advance of about 50 percent.

THE VOLUME BREAKOUT

The next market stage is the most comfortable for the buyer: It presents the opportunity to be fully invested on the long side, with everything appearing to be in gear for good long-term profits. The market has not only made a climax low and then tested it on light volume, it has shown strength by moving above resistance. It appears to be an early stage in a bull market, thereby suggesting that the move will last long enough for profits to be allowed to go long-term. In the example shown in Figure 11.1, the market has the single pullback test before starting up. Often there will be additional testing and base building before a move begins. Therefore, it is necessary to watch and wait for the breakout rather than try to second-guess it.

The stock action depicted on the Equivolume chart is the most classic of formations. It is, in fact, such a fundamentally important signal that it should never be ignored, regardless of the stage of the market. The formation consists of three stages: (1) a large decline in the stock, in which volume tends to be predominantly on the down moves, (2) a consolidation period in which the stock builds a substantial base, and finally (3) a move through the resistance with a power box. As we have seen before, a power box is a chart entry which has both heavier than normal volume and a wide spread between the high and the low. It is usually extremely apparent on an Equivolume chart as an entry with much more range and volume than any other recent entries. Never forget, however, that it must be going through a level of resistance in order to be a bullish sign.

Let us look at the chart for Merck as it approached the low of 1994 and then started a very strong up move in late 1994 through much of 1995 (Figure 11.4). At the beginning of the chart, in April of 1994, a fairly heavy volume reversal is made. In prior months, the volume moves had been primarily down, with rallies on lighter trading. Here, however, volume increases in the up direction for the first time since January. It is a sign that the stock is trying to turn around, but the base is too narrow to prompt any buying, since there is no *cause* for a substantial *effect*. Wide bases are usually needed if a good advance is to follow.

Figure 11.4 **VOLUME BREAKOUT—MERCK & CO. INC.**

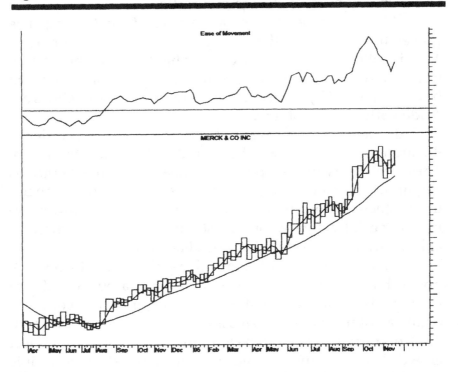

By August, though, the stock has tested the April low with lighter volume and small square boxes. Those months were enough to build a worthwhile base. Then, in September, we see a typical power box to the upside. Volume increases substantially as the stock advances, and the price spread widens. Most important, the power box penetrates the July high. It looks as though the stock is on its way.

In addition to the Equivolume characteristics that signaled a buy, note the two moving average lines. They were positive after the original low, then went negative on the light volume pullback, but crossed strongly in the plus direction just before the power box indicated a buy. Also, look at the upper oscillator: We see that the Ease of Movement moved into positive territory at the same time. It, too, was saying that the stock had seen a significant change of direction.

In Figure 11.5 we can see a close-up of the trading. The power box following the basing activity is very apparent. That is followed by a few weeks of light volume hesitation, but the move then resumes. From there on, the rallies tend to be accompanied by an increase in volume and the declines are made with lighter volume.

This Merck example was not carefully selected in order to illustrate the point. Power boxes out of bases are the norm. They are the strongest possible signal that an advance is beginning in a stock. They tell us that something has changed in the stock. A stock that was moving sideways is now moving upward. Evidently, for a reason that may not be discernable, a buying interest in this stock has developed.

I want to buy a stock that others also want to own. A power box tells me that someone else has a burning desire to own this stock and is willing to bid the price up in order to obtain a volume position. This is a time when I do not want to be a contrarian—I want to be with the crowd. But it is a select crowd. They are buying large amounts of the stock while it is near its low. Essentially, they are acting as contrarians, and I am following their lead.

Figure 11.5 **MERCK & CO. INC.—WEEKLY**

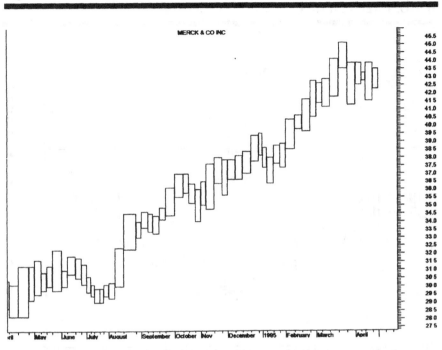

Since this is such a key part of any stock buying, let us look at another illustration before moving on. In addition, I suggest that readers look for power boxes on other illustrations throughout the book. Only on Equivolume charts do these boxes become apparent, and an investor should always be on the alert for power boxes. They are the quickest and easiest path to profitable trading.

Figure 11.6 shows the trading pattern of Armstrong World Industries in 1994 and 1995. Here we see a number of power boxes, first on the downside, then on the upside. The first upward power box is in January of 1995, creating the first good rally off the low. Until that time all the heavy volume

Figure 11.6 **POWER BOXES—ARMSTRONG WORLD INDUSTRIES—WEEKLY**

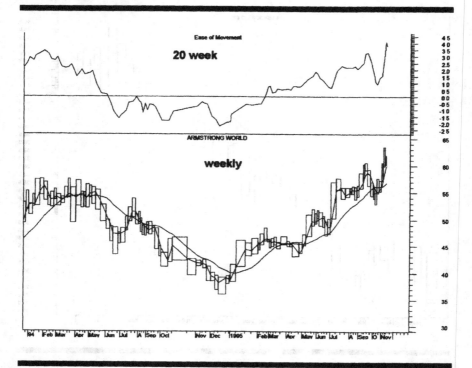

moves have been downward and within the descending pattern. Rallies tended to be lackluster, while declines had force. But the January rally is different—volume and range increase, and the descending pattern is destroyed.

With such a narrow base it is still too early to be a long-term buyer, however. We could surmise that the down move has ended, at least for the time being, but there is no real evidence yet that a lasting upward move has begun.

The more important power box is in May. By then a substantial base has formed. Looking across the chart, we can see that the base goes all the way back to October. That is enough base to justify a long advance. This power box is impressive, compared to the boxes that precede it. More important, it penetrates the highs of February with increasing volume and a widening spread. The stock loudly announces that it is starting an upward move. As is often the case, it has a light volume pullback and then goes much higher.

Whether to buy on the breakout or wait for the pullback always seems to be a dilemma. Sometimes a stock will have no pullback of any consequence but just continues to move up, while another pulls back to the breakout level on lighter volume before resuming the advance. I have found that the power box out of a base is more likely to have a pullback, while a later power box out of a continuation consolidation is somewhat less likely to have one. Therefore, on an early breakout I am more likely to put on half my intended position and wait for a possible pullback to complete my buying. On a breakout that comes later in the move, I am more likely to put on the entire position as soon as I see the breakout starting.

BUYING MIDWAY IN THE BULL MARKET

It would be pleasant to always have the opportunity to buy on breakouts from bases. As the bull market progresses, it is often possible to do so as interest shifts from one group to another. However, that is also likely to mean a shift toward lower-quality stocks. The early phases of a bull market usually see the best-quality stocks moving; emphasis later shifts to more speculative situations as the bull market ages. Part way through a bull market, the investor is likely to have excess cash after taking profits in stocks which reach objectives or start to act as though they are forming tops. The result is a need to buy new names in a market that is no longer near its lows and may be nearing a high. While the bull market is still in place, it is not desirable to hold a large amount of cash and thereby miss part of the rise.

The alternatives are either to buy stocks which are giving a classic signal of strength as they come out of bases late in the game or to buy stocks which are well above their lows. The second approach means that one is becoming a trend follower, but it keeps one in the better stocks. A stock that moves only late in the bull market may be doing so for a reason. It is being bought only because nothing else around appears cheap. I prefer to use at least part of my resources to buy stocks that are later in the cycle, in tune with the market, and do so when they give a new sign of strength after a consolidation. This means that I again look for power boxes after a consolidation, but now I eliminate the first requirement for a decline prior to the consolidation.

The chart for Banc One in Figure 11.7 illustrates this. The original *buy* signal is seen when it creates a power box at about the center of the chart, in February. Perhaps at the time so many stocks were breaking out that there was no money available for this one. Later, though, it goes through three consolidations, and each is followed by a new power box breakout through the top of the consolidation. They all lead to good gains. In each case the stock forms a strong base, pulls back on light volume, and then moves sharply higher with increasing volume and a widening spread. These are the same signs we looked for earlier in the bull market, except that then we also looked for a prior decline that had terminated with volume shifting to the buy side. This is an opportunity later in the bull move to buy a stock that has shown strength and gone through a new consolidation, and is again saying that it is headed higher.

BUYING LATE IN THE BULL MARKET

The last area to consider in a bull market is the topping that ends the bull market. It is a higher-risk area in which to be a

Figure 11.7 POWER BOXES AFTER CONSOLIDATION— BANC ONE CORP.

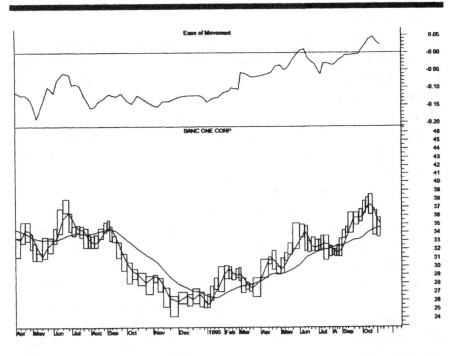

buyer, and a top should suggest extreme caution once recognized. After a series of upward moves and sideways consolidations, it is not easy to know if the latest consolidation is just another resting phase or the final top to the advance. If the consolidation in the market takes on the earmarks of a final top, be very hesitant about going long on individual issues.

As with the market, the characteristics of tops in particular stocks are slightly different than those of a consolidation. A consolidation, which is only a pause in the trend, is usually accompanied by lighter volume and the volume often decreases as the consolidation ages. On the other hand, a real top is more likely to see volume continue to be heavy, rather than dry up. In addition, major tops usually last longer—long enough to penetrate the ascending trend line that had been defining the up trend.

Imagine that you are climbing a very steep mountain. You pull yourself upward from ledge to ledge; each time you reach the comparative safety of any small shelf, you rest briefly to catch your breath and perhaps sit down for a brief time. When you finally pull yourself up over the last and steepest crag, using herculean effort to do so, you find yourself on the flat summit of the mountain. Now you are less likely to sit down, to settle back. You continue to expend effort as you walk across the crest and peer over the other side.

This, too, is the pattern of a climbing stock. It sits back and rests on each shelf, using as little energy as possible; but when it gets to the top, it trudges across the crest, expending energy but getting no higher.

In the chart of Champion International (Figure 11.8), we see such a series of rises and consolidations. After the original breakout from the base, early in the chart, there are a number of pullbacks. Note that each upward thrust is made with heavier volume and a widening of the price spread, while each hesitation is accompanied by decreasing volume and a downward slope to the prices. In each case, the stock reaches a ledge and sits down to rest.

Then, in July, we see the heaviest volume of the entire chart thus far, as the price moves to a new high. Also, the slope of the advance increases to an almost vertical move, in spite of the heavy volume. The signs of a possible top are evident. From that point, the stock moves sideways. It does not look the same as the earlier pullbacks, in that volume continues to be heavy and it moves laterally enough to penetrate the bottom of the steepest ascending trend line. The rally to the high, which fails, is made on lighter volume, suggesting a lack of power and, therefore, an inability to resume the advance. It is a low-volume test of the high-volume top and

Figure 11.8 **TOP FORMATION—CHAMPION INTERNATIONAL**

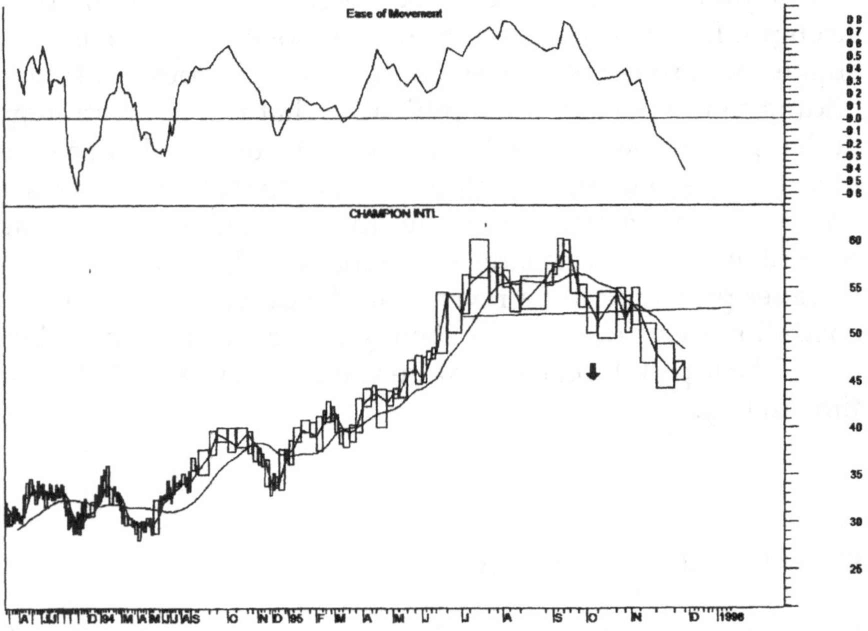

tells us that the stock is likely to be heading lower. The consolidation is far different from those that went before, and warns that a top could be in place. Finally, the downward move through support, marked with a down arrow, leaves little doubt—volume and spread increase as the support is penetrated. Additional evidence is provided by the two moving averages crossing to the downside and by the Ease of Movement going into minus territory shortly thereafter.

Buying stocks in a topping environment is dangerous. However, it is not always easy to know if it is a top or a consolidation. Therefore, I advise not buying any pullback except the first pullback off a low. Then it is likely to be at the start of an advance, but each later consolidation has a higher proba-

bility of being a top and is, therefore, that much more dangerous. If one stays with the principle of not buying a stock until
it has produced a power box, then one is buying only
strength. In earlier discussions of the move out of a base, we
suggested buying some stock on the breakout and then
adding to the position on a pullback. That is a good strategy
at that part of the market, but it should be used only in a situation where the move preceding the consolidation was a
decline. If the move preceding the consolidation was an
upward move, then it is later in the market phase, and there is
a higher probability of a reversal to the downside. If the consolidation turns out to be a shelf, not a crest, the power box
out of the top of the consolidation should tell us so. That is the
time to buy.

BUYING BEAR MARKET RALLIES

I see little justification for buying stocks in a bear market. Rallies in a bear market are likely to be very sharp and very short
lived, which makes them tempting. However, the risks are
larger than one should assume. In an obvious bear market, it
is safer to go short. Then one is investing in sympathy with
the market, rather than trying to make money by bucking a
trend. In a later chapter, we will discuss the short side of the
market and the popular belief that it is very risky. I believe the
risk of going against the trend is far higher than the prover-
bial risk of going short. The best alternative for a person who
is not of the temperament to be shorting stocks is to be out of
the market entirely.

Of course, there are mutual funds that are required to be
partially or fully invested at all times, regardless of market conditions. In this case the only choice is to look for strong areas in
a weak market. There are usually some groups of stocks buck-

ing the trend. As before, however, the buys should be based on power box moves out of substantial consolidations.

The first part of this chapter dealt with the first rally out of a climax in the market. Individual stocks also have climactic action, but, unlike the market, they are likely to see a number of false climactic formations on the way down. Therefore, one should not try to buy a move that appears to be a climax in an individual stock unless the market has said the same thing. Otherwise, the risk is too high that one is just buying a rally in a bear market. It is far safer to buy a stock that has built a substantial base and then given a convincing sign of strength. This strategy helps reduce the risk of buying in opposition to the market direction.

The Mechanics of Buying

Being responsible for investing large amounts of money—other people's money—I need to have a large number of stocks from which to make choices. The individual investor may not need to follow the 1,200 stocks in my basic universe in order to trade effectively. However, in today's age of easily available and cheap information, I think it is a mistake to follow and trade only a few stocks. The beauty of being a technician is the ability to look at a great number of issues easily. A fundamentalist who does the job well needs to look at so many details on each stock that it is impossible to effectively follow a great number of stocks in many different industries. The technician lets the market do the analysis, and translate it into prices and volume numbers, thereby enabling the study of far more stocks.

There is a more important reason to follow a large number of stocks than just having a bigger selection: It allows the investor to cover all the major industries. Historically, groups have tended to move together, so that even in a dull market there may be action in a single group, such as airlines or chemicals. A limited universe of charts could cause a trader to entirely miss an opportunity. Therefore, not only is it important to cover a large number of issues, but the list should be widely diversified. Probably the best way is to start with a basic list, such as the Standard & Poors 500, and then insert additional issues as they become interesting. Watching the most active lists for the NYSE and NASDAQ can often help to identify stocks that are gaining market attention. They can be added to the data list and then deleted later if the size of the list begins to get out of hand.

In recent years, data has become very inexpensive. Most data providers allow one to download data at a flat, low monthly rate, regardless of how many stock profiles are downloaded. They usually make the data available over a local phone number; so, at least in large U.S. metropolitan areas, the only limit to the size of a universe is the amount of computer time spent in downloading data each day. For end of day data I use Dial Data, which allows downloading everything one wants for about $30 each month.

Not many years ago, a technician needed to either manually chart as large a universe as time would allow or subscribe to a chart service. I still think it is worthwhile for a trader to chart a few items (perhaps market indices) by hand, in order to remain aware of the forces at work. But the proliferation of cheap and powerful computers has relegated the hand-drawn chart poster to a less-competitive position. With most traders able to look at hundreds of stocks instantly, the chartist who updates a few charts late into the night has a self-imposed disadvantage.

Born in the pre-war 1930s, I grew up in a world without computers. I have had to learn to live with them and use them to advantage. Occasionally, persons of my own vintage, who say that they are not computer literate, ask about my methods. The market is a competitive area where some are going to make money and others are going to lose. Being unwilling to use every possible tool in that arena is folly.

Almost every chart in this book was produced on a computer. I have a number of programs at my fingertips which allow me to look at hundreds of issues, inserting whatever parameters I wish. For some studies, especially the Arms Index work, I use a Lotus spreadsheet. I could, perhaps, use other programs, but over the years I have built a complete data library on these spreadsheets, with NYSE, ASE, and NASDAQ numbers going back to 1969.

For individual issues, I use Metastock for Windows. It contains Equivolume, Ease of Movement, and Volume Adjusted Moving Averages, done in a manner I find comfortable to use. Some of these features may be found in other charting programs, but they do not seem to be as easy to manipulate. I need to look at a large number of issues as quickly as possible. I am not interested in playing with the computer, I am interested in letting it do as much of the noncreative work as possible. The creative work is my part. I do not believe that today's computers can look at all the factors we are studying in this book and make as good a decision as I can. They do, however, make it possible for me to logically combine those factors more efficiently by providing as much data as I can assimilate in a legible and interpretable manner.

Almost every day I look at every stock in my universe. That does not mean that I linger over each issue. I don't need to. Years of experience allow me to glance at a chart and rapidly know if I want to look more closely. Anyone can develop that ability with a little practice. However, the computer program being used must allow the rapid review of a long list of stocks. I do not—and you should not—have the time or the desire to repeat steps once they are established. For example, we have decided that the optimum Volume Adjusted Moving Averages we want to put on a weekly chart are 3-volume and 20-volume moving averages. I want software that allows me to make those choices just once, so I can flip through the universe without having to tell the computer the parameters for each new stock. Whatever software is used, that should be a requirement.

Looking through the universe in this manner, I first visually scan for chart patterns that interest me. This is somewhat a function of the current market. For example, if it is an up market that has been in effect for a long time, I look for the type of breakouts from consolidations that are typical for that sort of market. I know that it is unlikely to find many issues breaking out from a base at that time, so opportunities are going to come from stocks that have had a consolidation and are starting a new up leg.

On the other hand, the classic down-base-breakout pattern does not go by unnoticed. Even late in a rising scenario, a part of the market may be acting differently, presenting classic buy opportunities.

After the first scan, jotting down interesting symbols, I go back and look much more closely at each candidate, paying attention to such other indicators as moving averages and Ease of Movement.

I scan the entire universe using weekly based charts. That gives an inventory of ideas—stocks that are developing a good longer-term pattern. For a stock to be a good shorter-term buy, it should first have a good longer-term pattern. The long-term moves are the dominant forces in the stock, and are therefore more reliable. What appears to be a desirable pattern on a short-term basis can be destroyed by the overriding force of the longer-term action. Therefore, the five-day chart is the first filter, and is often the determining factor in the selection of a stock for the portfolio.

This is not to say that one cannot trade from the patterns seen on a shorter-term chart. One of the fascinating things about these charts is that they produce rather similar patterns, so the same rules apply whether looking at long-term or short-term charts. For example, using Metastock Real Time programs and the Signal intraday data flow, it is possible, to produce Equivolume charts where each box represents just a few minutes of trading. If the stock or commodity is active enough to produce a steady flow of price and trade information, the chart will look amazingly like a daily or weekly chart. The same forces of supply and demand work at all levels; so, in response to those forces, volume will expand or contract and prices will move rapidly or slowly in a manner similar to that seen in a larger time frame. In the parlance of physicists, the market appears to be *fractal*.

However, the smaller the pattern, the more subject it is to becoming the victim of the larger pattern. The longer-term charts reflect the more powerful forces at work in the marketplace and mask the smaller swings. A short-term chart allows one to see those smaller swings and trade them. But the trader should never forget the longer-term pressures that can bias, or even negate, the short-term moves. It is for that reason that I look first at the longer-term charts and then move down to the short-term work. It is really an extension of the reasoning we used in deciding to understand the position and direction of the market before looking at individual stocks.

After choosing buy candidates from the overall list, it is necessary to look at the shorter-term picture. For that, a daily chart is usually the most helpful. There is a possibility that the weekly chart, in showing the major trends, has masked something important. For example, a stock may appear to have moved down with heavy volume on the weekly chart, whereas it becomes apparent on the daily chart that most of the volume came in on a single-day upsurge, and the bunching of data on the weekly chart covered over that detail. Knowing this could help to avoid a bad decision. In addition, the daily chart may reveal a pullback after the breakout—a detail that could allow us to buy at a better price. Of particular importance is the ability to more closely observe the way volume comes in on consolidations. The weekly chart often smooths out that information, making it less apparent.

The daily chart can also lead to more timely decisions. The move that eventually shows itself on the weekly chart may be apparent earlier on the daily work. For example, let us look at Figure 12.1, which is a weekly chart of St. Jude Medical for late 1993 through 1995. The first real sign of strength occurs in July 1994, the high-volume-box market indicated by the first up arrow. It is obviously a powerful breakout above the series

Figure 12.1 **ST. JUDE MEDICAL—WEEKLY**

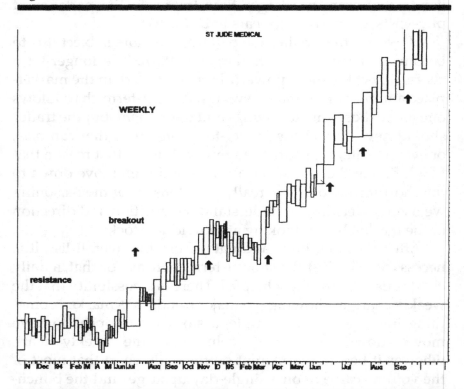

of highs shown by the horizontal line. It is a classic move— very hard to miss, even quickly browsing through a very large universe of stocks. It is even followed by a light-volume pullback, allowing the trader to buy at least part of the position at a better price. After that initial breakout, the volume continues to come in on advances and dry up on declines. Note the other up arrows on this chart: Each is a move through a resistance area, each is a power box, and each is preceded by a light-volume consolidation. Throughout the long advance, volume repeatedly indicates the direction.

Figure 12.2 is a daily chart of the same stock, but covers only the first breakout. The power box that got our attention

Figure 12.2 **ST. JUDE MEDICAL—DAILY**

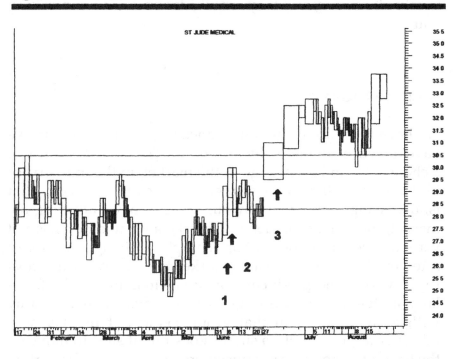

on the weekly chart is actually a combination of five boxes, including the up box marked 3 and the box after it. Looking at the weekly information, one would buy around the 32½ level and then on the pullback around 31.

But, based on the daily information, the two earlier boxes marked 1 and 2 are both power boxes through resistance, indicating a change taking place. An aggressive trader might do some buying there. More important, however, the real breakout day is on 3—it is not necessary to wait until the following day to know that a move is beginning.

In terms of the eventual move in the stock this is not a huge difference in price; nevertheless, the daily chart would be helpful in fine-tuning the buying. The three horizontal lines on the daily chart show that three resistance areas are involved, not one, and they are all penetrated in a convincing manner.

SEARCH PROGRAMS

We have recognized the importance of power boxes, but we have not yet examined why they occur. They occur because of a change. It can be a change in the market, in the industry, or in the issue itself, and the change can be overt or covert. That is, the change can be an obvious piece of news affecting the market, industry, or issue; or it can be a change that has not yet surfaced in the news. For example, a change in interest rates might cause the entire market to rally, carrying most issues with it and producing breakouts in many stocks. Similarly, all the drug stocks might start to advance in sympathy with a single stock in that group being put in play as a takeover target. Finally, a single stock might start to move on the basis of a product announcement or an earnings report. In all these cases the reason is fairly obvious, although the direction of movement or extent of movement may be a surprise; it depends upon the psychological effect of the announcement rather than the announcement itself.

On the other hand, many power boxes are created with no apparent cause. This does not mean that there is no cause—there is. It means that someone knows something that is not general knowledge in the investment community. A cynic might say prices are being moved with volume on the basis of inside information, although we know the SEC has made sure that cannot happen. But, for whatever reason, every power box has a cause, and often the cause is not immediately apparent. When we search through our hundreds of issues looking for buying opportunities, we are really looking for change.

We are searching for stocks that have come under accumulation or reaccumulation and are therefore acting differently than they had been—a sideways move that has become an upward move.

A good computer program can be extremely helpful in searching for opportunities. It is possible to exhibit a chart for every stock that is acting in a specific fashion. I do this daily— I want to see any stock that formed a box on the prior day with an area at least twice as large as any of the preceding boxes over the last month. A number of stocks will be displayed. Some will be obvious, based upon well-publicized events; others may be mysterious moves with no apparent cause. The mysterious ones are often the most interesting, because they are saying that someone is accumulating the stock for no apparent reason. Perhaps they know something I do not! If so, they have created unusual price and volume action that is atypical for that stock. They have left their fingerprints on the stock, and we are dusting the market for fingerprints.

Of course, every stock that shows up on the search is not a buy candidate. It must be an upside move through resistance, with a tall box for its width. Many qualifiers are likely to be short wide boxes, and many others are down rather than up moves. The power boxes to the downside may, of course, be short sale candidates, which we will consider later.

TIMING THE BUY

Suppose that we have decided to buy a particular stock. It has produced a great-looking power box, after a long consolidation. The resistance has been convincingly penetrated, and it has even pulled back a little on lighter trading. Today is the day to buy! But do we just put in a market buy order on the opening? I prefer to see the opening of the market and get a feel for the direction of the market and the particular stock. Then I usually use a limit order for my protection. I often buy large enough amounts to affect the market and harm myself, so I prefer to have a limit, above which I will not buy the stock. I am not trying to shave the price, I am protecting myself from a surprise. I am willing, however, to buy around the current level, since it is a stock I have decided I want to own.

Since the technical work has said that it should be bought here and now, I am not willing to miss an opportunity by trying for a fractionally better price. If it is a heavily traded stock, and the purchase is small relative to the stock's volume, a market order is not a bad idea. The main point is that the decision has been made to own the stock, so being too cute on price can be a mistake.

When to place the order can be important, however. Market action can make quite a bit of difference in the price paid. Consequently, I suggest that the trader watch the overall market and ascertain its direction before jumping in. I like to look at the Arms Index for this. When used this way, the actual number is not as important as its change. There is a tendency for the index to lead the market. Therefore, if the index starts to move lower (which means it is becoming more bullish), it suggests that the market is likely to move higher in response. Such action is a reason to go ahead and start buying, hoping to get the stock before it and the market move higher. Conversely, an index that is becoming progressively higher suggests that the market is likely to weaken, prompting me to hold off on buying and try to catch it at better prices. In a dull market with the index staying about the same, I just go ahead and do my trades.

Another clue from the Arms Index during the trading day is the *extreme reading*. We know that a normal AI is around 1.00, and numbers between .75 and 1.25 are not unusual. Sometimes, however, the index will go very far in one direction or the other, then stop moving in that direction. It is usually telegraphing a turn. Suppose, for example, that the market has dropped 42 Dow points during the morning, but now seems to be holding in that area. In the meantime, the index has risen to 2.50 and now seems to have quit going higher. Selling appears to be overdone on a short-term basis. It is a time to initiate the buys that have already been decided upon.

A similar extreme in the index in the other direction might be a .50 reading and an up market that is hesitating. This would suggest holding off on buying, in anticipation of a pullback.

HOW MUCH TO BUY

Earlier we spoke of buying a partial position on the breakout and then completing the buying on the pullback. That is often effective on the original breakout from a large base, but it is less effective on a continuation breakout from a consolidation, because a pullback is quite a bit less likely. Remember, however, that the stock has qualified as a buy, and trading techniques, while helpful, should not stand in the way of owning the stock. If only part of a position is bought on the breakout and no pullback is then seen, the trader should complete the buying, even at higher prices, rather than miss owning a full position of a strong stock.

Diversification or concentration? That is not an easily answered question. A mutual fund is diversified because that is part of its function. It spreads the risk by owning many issues. Usually, depending upon the nature of the fund, it also spreads the holdings over many industries. An individual may not have the resources or the time to own and follow a large portfolio. Diversification lowers the risk, but also lowers the potential rewards. No one stock or industry, even when it does very well, can greatly impact a widely diversified portfolio.

Years ago, when I was a rookie broker, a man who was to become, for a short time, my biggest customer, once deposited a large amount of money in his margin account and told me he would buy and sell exactly as I advised. I immediately suggested that we buy about 20 stocks which I felt were acting as they should to be attractive buys.

"Wait," he said. "There is only one ground rule. I want to own only one stock at a time, and the entire buying power goes into that issue."

This we did, with amazing success. Whether the fact that I was putting so much money into one situation made me more astute, or I was just lucky, I don't know, but I could do little wrong. After only a few months the customer called, and told me to put all of his new wealth into municipal bonds. He retired on the income and never, to my knowledge, traded stocks again.

That is an extreme. I feel, however, that wide diversification is for long-term investors, not active market participants. If, for example, copper stocks are the best-acting stocks at a given time, a trader should try to capitalize on that, rather than have a large part of the available assets in oils which are not participating. Since we know we cannot always be right on each stock we pick, diversification among a number of issues is helpful. But that does not mean buying less-attractive issues in order to be diversified. Putting all our eggs in one basket may be extreme, but one egg in each of a hundred different baskets may be equally extreme. We should not have our eggs in more baskets than we can comfortably watch. There should be a continual monitoring of every position, in order to know when to sell. That monitoring is the subject of the next chapter.

Now You Own It

When you bought that stock in the last chapter, you were able to make a very logical and unemotional decision. It was just another company, among hundreds in your universe. But it was acting right. The volume was heavy where it should have been and light where it should have been and both volume and price spread increased impressively as it sprang up through resistance. Now, however, the relationship has become more personal. It is not just another stock, it is *your* stock, and you laid your reputation on the line by buying it. If it does not do as you expect, you will be proven wrong and have to answer to somebody, if only yourself, for a bad decision. You are emotionally involved, and, as we have seen, emotional decisions are the trader's worst enemy. In the case of buying a stock, emotional involvement tends to swing one to a position of excessive optimism. Prior to buying the stock, fear and greed were in equilibrium, but the act of buying brings in an optimistic outlook which can be dangerous. The stricture of *caveat emptor* takes on a different meaning: The buyer must beware—but of her- or himself, not of others.

One particular danger is the creation of additional emotional involvement. It is bad enough to explain an error to oneself without having to also explain it to others. Therefore, unless it is absolutely necessary, no other person should be told what has been bought. Of course, a money manager must tell her employers what she has bought, but an individual investor need tell no one but his broker. It should not be cocktail party conversation, since the very revelation of what one is doing creates a later need to explain either success or failure. An extraneous factor is introduced that can only warp judgment.

The truly unemotional decision is reached by acting as though the stock is *not* owned. Continually ask, "If I didn't own this stock, would I buy it now?" A *no* answer leads to the second question: "Would I be willing to short this stock?" A *yes*, of course, demands that the stock be immediately sold. A *no* suggests that the stock is still acting okay, but not as well as might be hoped. That leads to the third question: "Is there some place my money could do better?"

These three questions must be answered in a detached manner, and the answers cannot be ignored or rationalized. A stock that is no longer a buy need not necessarily be sold, but it should be watched closely. A stock that is obviously acting weak should never be held.

Price should play no direct part in a decision to sell. The market neither knows nor cares what you paid for a stock, and that price has no direct bearing on what the stock is going to do in the future. The only pertinent information is the activity of the stock. Whether we sell at a loss or a gain may be very important to our finances, but it should not be important in our decision making. That is not to say that the decision to take a profit is identical to the decision to get out of a losing position before it becomes worse. But the difference is based upon the fact that the stock is in a different position, not that we have a profit or a loss. When taking a profit, the stock must be farther from the base than it was when we established the position. Therefore, it must be later in the cycle and, hence, more vulnerable. That leads to an earlier sell decision, not waiting for as much evidence of a turnaround before selling. On the other hand, if the stock is below where we bought it, it is also nearer its base and perhaps is nearer support. Under those circumstances, one is likely to be a little bit more lenient.

OBJECTIVES

It has been repeatedly stressed that the width of a base is a major consideration in establishing a long position. A stock with a wide base is likely to produce a better profit than a stock with a narrow base. Actually, there is a much closer relationship between the size of a consolidation and the extent of a move—a direct volume-to-volume relationship. The amount of volume in a base is usually close to the volume expended in the ensuing advance, and the amount of volume in a top is usually close to the volume expended in the ensuing decline. It is a direct cause and effect relationship: The number of shares accumulated during the building of a base is the same as the number used up in the advance which follows. Let us look at an example.

Since we are talking about volume measurements, and since volume is constant along the horizontal axis of an Equivolume chart, we will do all our measuring in the horizontal direction. In Figure 13.1 we see a rather narrow base to the far left, marked measurement 1 (m1). The distance between the two outward-pointing arrows is the accumulation area of the base. There appear to be two walls to the base, the first on the final breakdown and the second on the breakout above resistance. This distance between the walls is the base. The advance after the breakout can be expected to last until about the same amount of volume has traded as was traded in the base. We measure that distance laterally, as at the area marked objective 1 (o1). The size of the base gives us a good idea how much we can expect from the stock, and alerts us to look for signs that it is time to take profits.

The next consolidation is indicated as m2, and turns out to be a top. It is much wider than the prior base, saying that more volume is likely to be expended in the ensuing decline. By measuring the same distance laterally we find objective 2 (o2), which turns out to be very near the lowest point reached by the stock. Finally, we have another accumulation area, des-

Figure 13.1 VOLUME OBJECTIVES—SMITHS FD & DRUG

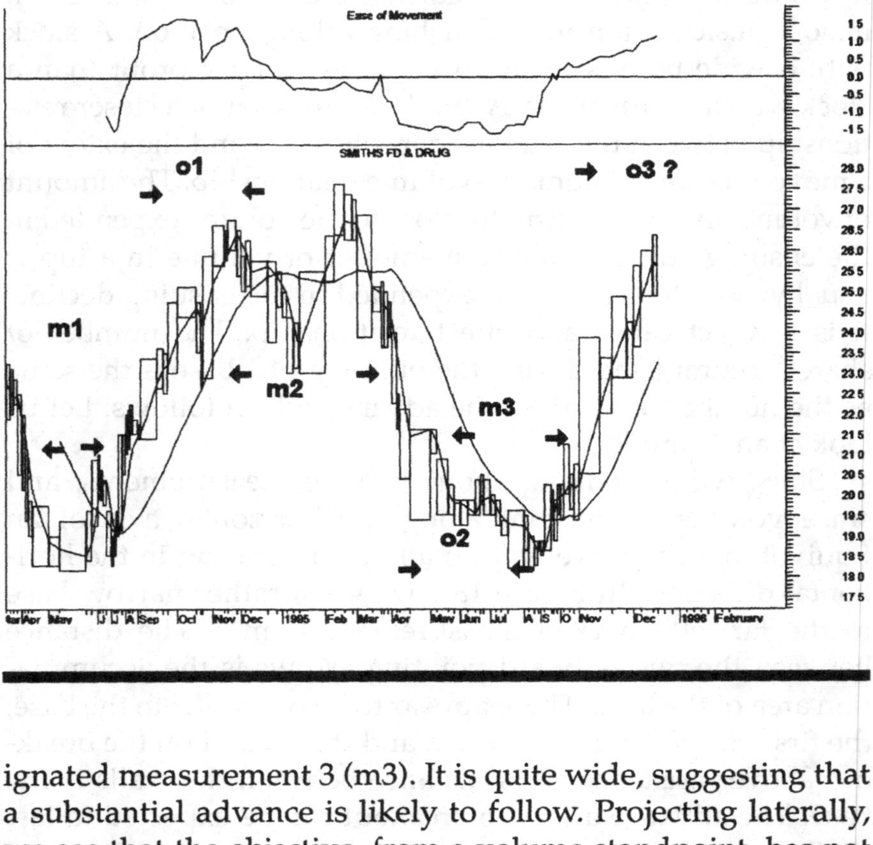

ignated measurement 3 (m3). It is quite wide, suggesting that a substantial advance is likely to follow. Projecting laterally, we see that the objective, from a volume standpoint, has not yet been reached at the end of the chart. That is a clue that the advance has farther to go, and would keep one from selling too soon.

After buying a stock, it is worthwhile to measure the base and then mark off a similar volume distance to the right, to establish how much volume is likely to be used in the runup. We often refer to a stock as *having used up its base* or *still having more top to work off*. The width of a consolidation should not be the determining factor in closing out a position, but it should serve as a warning when the objective is neared.

CYCLES

Of course, if we combine a number of consolidations followed by declines and then consolidations followed by advances, it produces a series of up and down cycles, or waves. These waves tend to be quite regular on a volume basis. That is, on an Equivolume chart they are likely to be equidistant, regardless of the time elapsed. If volume is light, it takes more time to reach the next crest of a wave; if volume is heavy, we get there sooner. This is a result of our basic premise that *the market does not know what time it is*. Time is a human measurement, while volume is a stock market measurement. A market advance will progress until a certain number of shares have been bought—and it does not matter how long that takes. Similarly, a decline will go on until a certain number of shares have been sold, regardless of the elapsed time. If the same number of shares tend to change hands in each upward and downward move, the swings begin to take on a wave pattern, with the wave crests or troughs equidistant from one another.

In the chart for Biomet (Figure 13.2), the wave action is very obvious. The wave crests at the beginning, center, and a little before the end of the chart are spaced very evenly across the chart. Owning the stock and seeing this pattern, the last top would be expected and anticipated. That, combined with the crossing of the two moving average lines, would probably prompt some profit taking.

One should always be aware of the cyclicality of a stock. It provides a reliable clue as to whether a move is likely to go farther. In Figure 13.3 we see a stock that exhibits good cyclicality—USF&G.

The first top is seen early in January 1995. Then, in May, a second top forms with all the Equivolume earmarks of a reversal to the downside: volume top followed by light volume test, cross of the moving averages, Ease of Movement going negative. The decline does occur, followed by the start

Figure 13.2 CYCLES—BIOMET INC.

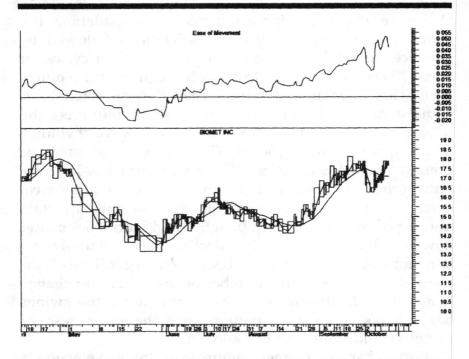

of another advance in July. Volume again increases on the upside as the longer-term up pattern resumes.

Then, in August, we see some square entries, right after the volume penetration of the May highs. Ease of Movement is erratic and the two moving average lines whipsaw. It looks as though a top may be forming. However, the cycle would imply that it is early for a top to form. If the volume is to complete a cycle similar to the prior cycle, then it still has some way to go. This consideration is enough to prompt more of a waiting attitude.

The stock does go to a higher high in October, at which time the cycle consideration has been satisfied. Again there is a volume top followed by a light volume test, the moving

Figure 13.3 **CYCLES—USF&G CORP.**

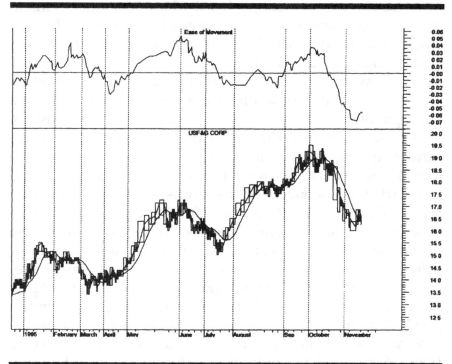

average lines cross decisively to the minus side, and the Ease
of Movement also goes negative. Because of the cycle considerations this becomes a much more believable top than
the August highs and is a time to sell.

SELLING ON CONSOLIDATIONS

As we have seen, the way in which a consolidation progresses
is a clue as to whether the advance is ending or merely resting. This can be very helpful in knowing whether to sell out a
long position. To reiterate, the up leg usually ends with heavy

volume and may also be a square entry. Then the stock tends to move sideways or somewhat lower. If volume begins to drop as the sideways move progresses, it suggests that the stock is not through with its advance. Constant heavy trading is more likely if a top is forming.

The way we act in response to the start of a consolidation depends upon our position. If the consolidation follows a strong move that has put us in a profit position, we must try to ascertain whether the width of the base justifies more upward movement or whether the stock is near the predetermined objective. If the stock has reached the objective and has started to encounter obvious resistance, I see no reason not to take the profit. If the consolidation is a top, as the volume measurement implies, then we are selling near the top of the move. On the other hand, if it is only a resting phase prior to another upward move, the stock can always be rebought. I have no problem rebuying a stock, even at a higher price, if it is saying it is a buy. Since a stock usually spends a good deal more time in consolidations than it does in advances or declines, getting out as a consolidation begins frees up money that would be idle during a consolidation of uncertain outcome.

If the stock has not yet reached or neared its objective, it is often worthwhile to wait and see the nature of the consolidation. The money may remain idle for some time, but the odds favor an eventual resumption of the advance. The stock was originally bought because of its very strong chart pattern, and it is still conforming to that pattern. Selling and rebuying may mean rebuying at a higher level and paying two commissions. As long as the consolidation progresses as expected, with decreasing volume and a small pullback, the position looks fine. If, instead, the volume does not decrease and the stock moves sideways far enough to penetrate the ascending trend line, it can be sold. Of course, a heavier volume drop through the bottom of the consolidation calls for an immediate closing of the position.

In Figure 13.4, we see a weekly chart of Amdahl as it makes a strong move and then turns down. The first up arrow shows the buy signal. The stock was coming out of a long base and produced a power box through resistance. The width of the base implied a lengthy advance. The second up arrow is another penetration of resistance and is followed by a pullback lasting five weeks. It comes so soon after the original breakout that it seems unlikely that the base has been used up; it tells us to wait and see, rather than take the profit. There are a number of other small pullbacks on the way up, but none come after a square heavy volume box; therefore, they are not bothersome. By the time the large downward box (marked with the first down arrow) is made we may

Figure 13.4 **VOLUME OBJECTIVES—AMDAHL CORP.**

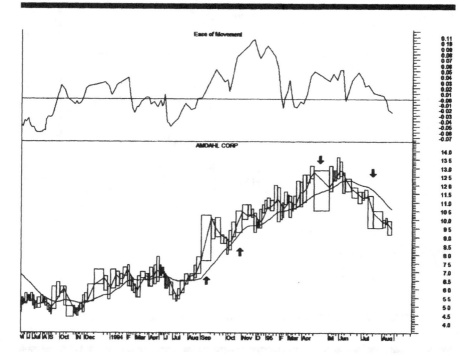

already be a little apprehensive, because it is getting late in the move and the base may be about used up. In this case there is no warning before that heavy volume down box to suggest that the advance is ending. The box itself penetrates the up trend, however, and emphatically informs us that a change has occurred. Volume is now in the down direction. It is a time to sell. It is not yet a time to go short, because no wide top has formed, but the up move has become very suspect. Later, at the second down arrow, one might want to sell the stock short.

In Figure 13.5, the resting phases and continuations are quite typical. They, too, are early enough in the move to sug-

Figure 13.5 **TOP—TORO CO.**

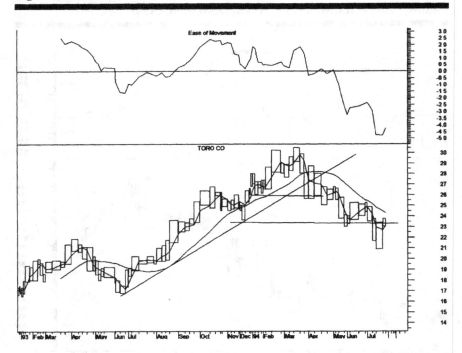

gest that more strength is to follow. The top is quite different, however. Volume remains quite heavy as the stock moves sideways. Then the two moving average lines cross to the minus side, and the Ease of Movement goes negative. At the same time, we see a sharp downward move out of the consolidation and a penetration of the ascending trend line. One might take the profit as the top progresses, seeing that it is not acting as a minor pullback would be expected to. If not, however, the breakdown box gives an unmistakable signal that it is time to move on.

TYPICAL TOPPING FORMATIONS

We have said nothing, so far, about some traditional formations that technicians constantly refer to, such as the head and shoulders top, the triple top, and the double top. Actually, all of these are simply manifestations of the same points we have been referring to in studying consolidations.

A head and shoulders top is a consolidation in which three peaks are made, with the center peak higher than the other two. If they were all the same height, we would just call it a triple top and forget the more specific name. The more important fact is that in a head and shoulders top we expect to see a decrease in volume from top to top. That is, we see a heavy-volume top and two lighter-volume tests. As we have observed before, final tops have this characteristic.

I believe it is much more productive to look at every stock in terms of being in either a consolidation phase or a moving phase. If it is in a consolidation, then it must be observed closely to ascertain whether the consolidation is likely to be a resting phase in a continuing move or the terminal phase of a move.

SELLING A BAD POSITION

It would be nice to always be right, and to have every chart behave as well as the examples in a book. That is not, unfortunately, the case. Even charts that seem to be doing just as we anticipated will sometimes suddenly go against us. When that happens, there is no reason to let pride or hope stand in the way of getting out.

In the chart for Tambrands (Figure 13.6), we see just such a scenario. In the early part of the chart, volume is obviously to the downside, and the stock is in a decline. The first up arrow marks a change in the stock. For the first time in months, volume comes in on an advance instead of a decline.

Figure 13.6 **TAMBRANDS INC.**

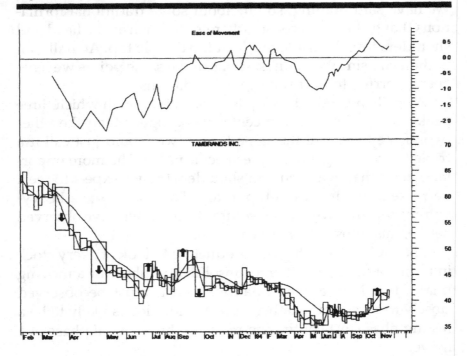

It is too early to buy, however; no base has formed, so no substantial rise is to be anticipated.

The second up arrow is a different story: It is a powerful move through resistance out of a strong base. It implies that a good up move is beginning. In the next two weeks, volume dries up somewhat as the stock pulls back. It looks like a textbook buy!

But then, after buying the stock, look what happens the very next week: It drops down to the bottom of the old consolidation with heavy volume and a widening price spread. At this point, it would be easy to rationalize—to say that the old support has not been broken and that the consolidation is resuming. But, even if that were true, it is not the chart pattern we bought, and not the promising stock it had been. There is now no reason to own that stock, and it should be immediately sold.

As we see, the stock does continue to go down for almost a year, but even if it did not, there is no reason to own a stock that appears, at best, to be in a consolidation. Not when our money could be in another stock that is in an up move.

A stock should be sold when its action is wrong, regardless of the profit or loss involved. I do not believe in setting a percentage loss at which a stock should be closed out, since such a mechanical approach does not take into consideration the chart action of the stock. Neither, for that reason, do I believe in a trailing stop. On the other hand, a well-thought-out stop that recognizes what sort of a move constitutes an obvious breakdown can be helpful, since it reduces the likelihood of making an emotional decision later.

I do not try to second-guess prices in closing out a losing position. I like to start getting out as soon as I see that I am wrong. Of course, as in buying, the Arms Index can be helpful in timing the move, and market direction should be taken into consideration. These tools should not override the decision to correct an error, but they may help to mitigate the loss.

Selling a position is a more difficult decision than establishing a position. It is like judging a horse show when one of the horses is your own. You can no longer be objective.

I believe that most of us are more likely to sell a stock with profit too soon and sell a stock with loss too late. Therefore, I suggest purposely forcing oneself to be patient with stocks that are doing well and very impatient with stocks that are acting wrong. This may offset the natural inclination to rationalize a loss or quickly grab a small gain, regardless of what the technical picture is saying. In addition, the questions "Would I buy this stock if I didn't own it?" and "Would I sell this stock short?" are very helpful in avoiding wishful thinking.

Selling a stock short is a far less emotional decision than selling a long position, because it is a new decision wherein one does not have to deal with being right or wrong. In the next chapter we discuss short sales.

Looking for Short Sales

It is generally accepted that selling a stock short is much more risky than buying a stock. This is not true. The assertion that short selling is dangerous is based in part upon the fact that one is required to do the shorting in a margin account, and that in itself scares many people: "Your uncle Henry was trading on margin in 1929, and was wiped out in the crash!" In reality, however, the reason it is done in a margin account is that a loan is involved—but a loan of stock rather than money. In selling a stock short, you sell something that you do not own and, therefore, are unable to deliver. The only way to provide the stock to the person who purchases it—and expects to receive it—is to borrow it from someone else. That is a loan; therefore, it is a margin transaction. A person who is apprehensive about trading with borrowed money may prefer to sell short only as much stock as he or she has cash available to buy back; the trader is then unleveraged and can treat the sale as though it were not a margin transaction.

A second reason given for not selling short is that a stock can go against one infinitely far in a short, whereas in a long position one can lose only what is invested. In other words, if you short a stock at 50, it can go up forever, and all that movement is a loss; but if you buy a stock at 50 it can sink only to zero and can lose no more than you invested. Certainly, that is mathematically true, but we are not talking about blindly taking positions and never looking at them again. The principles put forth in this book should make it very difficult for anyone to watch a stock move very far in the wrong direction without correcting the error.

Moreover, we know that most market moves are slower in the up direction than they are in the down direction. A stock tends to slowly work its way higher, then drop very rapidly. This means that a person who buys a stock at the right time watches profits accumulate slowly; whereas, if the stock drops, the loss occurs very rapidly, giving less time to correct the error. On the other hand, the short seller sees a winning position develop rapidly and a losing position develop slowly, allowing more time to correct the mistake. From that standpoint, a short is somewhat safer than a buy.

The third argument against short selling is more valid. Historically, the market has risen much more than it has declined. A Dow that once was below 100 has risen well above 5,000 over the years. This says that the odds have favored the buy side of the market over the short-selling side. Yes, but there have still been many bear markets and, as we saw in earlier chapters, there are many ways of knowing it is a bear market. Why try to fight a strong down trend in the market and struggle to find the few issues that may be bucking that trend? In the absence of any knowledge of the market direction, the assumption must be made that the market goes up more than it goes down. But, with the ability to ascertain the nature of the market, there are times when selling short is the safest way to continue to participate in the market.

It is often said that short selling is for speculators, not investors. In a way that is true, in that a holder of a stock collects dividends while a short seller is charged for dividends. This means that someone whose aim is income rather than capital gains should not be going short. But anyone who trades in the market with the intention of buying at a lower price than the price at which the stock is sold should be as willing to go short as long. Whether one is a buyer or a short seller, the desire is to sell at a higher price than the buy price. In going long, one buys before selling, whereas in going short, one sells before buying.

WHAT TO SELL

In most respects shorting a stock calls for a chart pattern that is the mirror image of what we look for in a buy. The price should move down out of a consolidation area with increasing volume and a widening price spread. That creates a power box downward.

Let us look at Figure 14.1, a weekly chart of McDermott International in 1993 and part of 1994. It moves steadily higher in the first half of 1993, with volume increasing on each upswing and declining on each pullback. The first clue that the stock might be encountering a reversal to the downside is the square entry in early August, which proves to be the top of the move. After that square box there are two more weeks of trading in the same range, spreading the sideways area laterally.

The following two weeks are an important warning. Volume increases as the price declines. It is the first time that has been seen. Then, after a light-volume attempt to rally, the volume again picks up as the stock drops down through support. That support is indicated by the horizontal line coming from the July lows. The breakdown box is indicated by the down arrow. It is that breakdown which gives the signal to sell the stock short.

There can be little question that the stock has rolled over to the downside. The ascending trend line has been penetrated, the two moving average lines have crossed in the negative direction, and volume is flowing in the sell direction. The trader might wait for a little rally, since one is so often seen after the first breakdown. Or a partial position could be put on immediately, with the intention of adding to the short on a

Figure 14.1 **DOWNSIDE REVERSAL—MCDERMOTT**
INTERNATIONAL

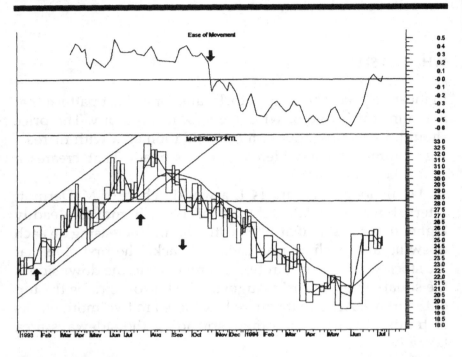

rally. A few weeks later the Ease of Movement also goes negative, confirming the validity of the position.

If one was looking for a traditional formation the picture on this chart could be interpreted as a head and shoulders, with the first shoulder in July, the head in August, and the second shoulder the light-volume rally in September. The move that we call the power box to the downside (marked with a down arrow) could be called a penetration of the neckline.

The next chart (Figure 14.2) is even more dramatic in its breakdown. Niagara Mohawk had been trading in a sideways range with unimpressive volume. There is good support evi-

Figure 14.2 VOLUME BREAKDOWN—NIAGARA MOHAWK

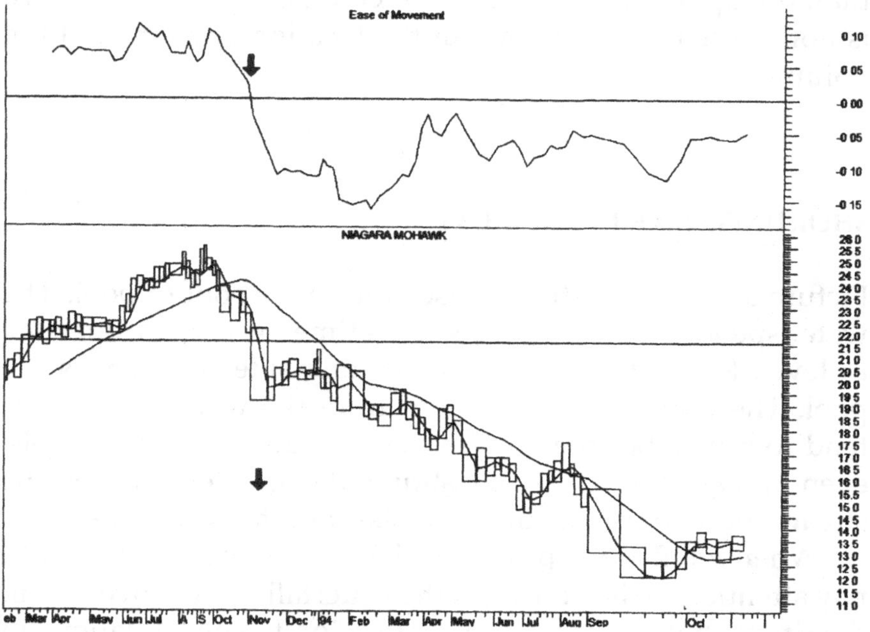

dent in the 21½ area, where the horizontal line has been
inserted. In November it suddenly drops through that support with heavy volume and a widening spread—a power
box downward. This coincides with the crossing to negative
territory of the Ease of Movement, and comes well after the
two moving average lines have given a *sell* indication. It is an
unmistakable sign that the stock should be sold short.

After the breakdown there is a lighter-volume rally that
takes the price back up to just about the horizontal line—old
support has now become resistance. Note, in this case, that
the top is not a double or triple top, but merely a rolling
over. The top, however, is obvious once the power box to the

downside appears. In addition, prior to that box the volume has already started to be seen on the down moves rather than the up moves. The key to catching this profitable move is not the shape of the top but the location and effect of the volume.

SHORTING LATER IN THE MOVE

Picture a mountain stream cascading from pool to pool. The water spends a comparatively short time dropping from level to level. Most of the time it is drifting sideways across the pool. The dramatic effect comes from the waterfalls, so we tend to remember them more than we do the quieter pools, even though the pools constitute the greater part of the stream. But the fish are in the pools—not the waterfalls!

When we fish for profits in the stock market we need to pay attention to the pools, not the waterfalls. The moves are in the drops, but we need to pay attention to consolidations in order to recognize the opportunities. We catch the big trout in the deep, quiet pools, not in the cascades.

As a stock declines, it tends to have repeated and regular consolidations that present additional shorting opportunities. They have the same appearance as consolidations in a bull move, in that volume tends to decrease markedly and they go counter to the trend—in this case, up. In fact, consolidations during a decline tend to be more regular than similar pullbacks during an advance. If a stock breaks down out of a top, but the original opportunity to short is not acted upon, there are usually repeated chances to go in later. Let us look at a typical such decline. Figure 14.3 charts Lowes in 1994 to 1995.

In the first two-thirds of the chart, each advance is accompanied by heavy volume, as indicated by the up arrows. Then, in December, the situation changes completely. For the

Figure 14.3 **SHORTING SIGNALS—LOWES COS INC.**

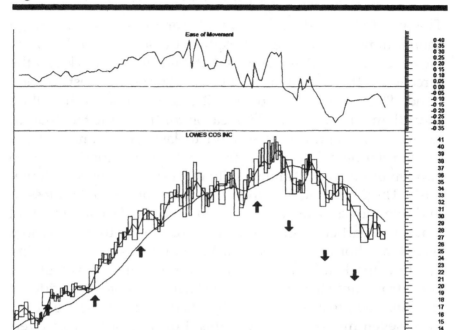

first time in many months, volume comes in on a down week. In addition, the ascending trend is violated and the moving averages go negative. It is a sign of weakness that could be interpreted as a *sell short* signal. If one did not act immediately, however, the next rally would be an attention-getter because of the lack of volume. It takes on the appearance of a typical consolidation in a down-moving stock. As the chart progresses we see two other similar signals and opportunities, also indicated by down-pointing arrows. The stock is in a downward cascade that gives repeated chances to short the stock.

WHEN TO SELL SHORT

The time to buy a stock is in a bull market, but the time to go short is almost anytime except right at the start of a bull market. We have said in earlier chapters that it is important to know the direction of the market in order to avoid fighting an established trend. That is certainly true, but it is less important in selling short than it is in buying. The reason for this is the fact that up moves in the entire market tend to last longer and involve group rotation, while down moves in the entire market tend to happen more quickly and usually most stocks drop simultaneously. The group rotation is evident in up moves, but far less so in down moves. Therefore, one can short stocks even in a bull market as particular groups run out of momentum. It is more risky than shorting in a bear market, but not as risky as buying in a bear market. In mid-1995 the overall market was still in a very strong upward move, but the technology stocks suddenly encountered great resistance. They had led the advance of the prior seven months, but were ahead of the market and overdone. The bull market was not over, as could be seen in the broad averages, but the technology stocks were in trouble.

One of the leaders in the group was Intel. We see in Figure 14.4 that it ran sharply higher until July, when it suddenly traded unprecedented volume and made a reversal. Two weeks later it penetrated the ascending trend line and also penetrated support, with heavy volume and a wide spread. In November, the stock tried to resume its advance, but volume was lacking on the move, and it turned down well below the old high. There was money made on the short side of this stock in spite of the continuing up move in most stocks. Sector rotation had caught up with it, as money started to go to other groups.

At the start of a bull market the risks of going short are much higher than they are later in the move. As a strong up market begins, the strength is likely to be selective, with a few sectors leading the way and others doing nothing. However,

Figure 14.4 **REVERSAL PATTERN—INTEL CORP.**

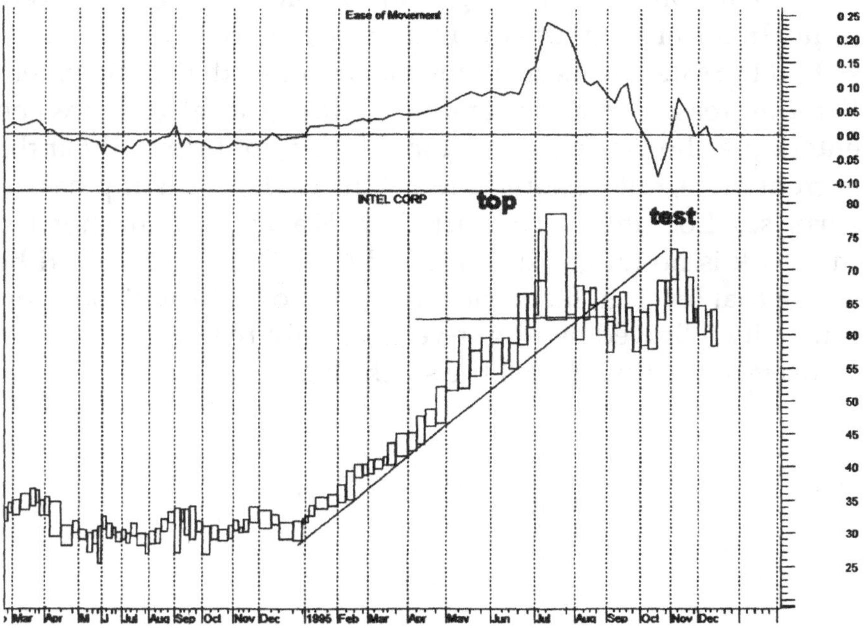

even the sectors that are not participating are unlikely to be moving down enough to justify the risk of establishing short positions. It is still too early for any groups to have had their moves and then started to give way to rotation. Consequently, the early stage of a major bull market is the one time when the possible rewards of a short position do not justify the risk.

HOW TO SELL SHORT

Selling short is not as easy as buying a stock because of the *up tick rule:* One is not allowed to short a stock at a lower price than the prior trade, in order to stop short sellers from accelerating a decline. It means that you can only sell into a rising price. This presents a danger to anyone placing a market order. In the absence of any up moves, the price can fall away, so that the sale is done at a much lower price than anticipated. For this reason it is imperative to use a limit order when entering a short-sale transaction. It need not be exactly at the current price, but it should protect the trader from unpleasant surprises. Looking at the chart, there is a level where shorting the stock is no longer such a good deal. The limit should be above that level. In fact, since the first move through support is usually followed by a light-volume rally, that rally can often be used as the time to sell the stock short.

Closing Out Short Positions

To carry the analogy of the mountain stream a little further, as it cascades downward it tends to form a series of pools, only to tumble over the lip of the basin and drop again. There comes a time, however, when the bottom of the cascade is reached. Often that is signaled by a much larger waterfall, a precipitous plunge into a much larger and deeper pool. A violent and tumultuous cataract often ends the decline. The frothy power of the downward move is confused and noisy. So, too, is the end of a drop in stocks, very often. After a series of downward cascades, prices seem to slide over the lip of a vertical drop and plunge into a frothy maelstrom of activity. This is different from the consolidations on the way down, and it signals a capitulation. Holders are dumping the stock indiscriminately, paying little attention to price in a headlong rush to get out.

A very heavy volume decline—essentially a power box down, but one that comes late in the move—is a warning that the move may be terminating. It is quite different from the typical topping action, which is more likely to be a rounding over as buying loses its momentum. An upward move seems to quit with a drop in momentum, whereas a decline more typically ends with high momentum. The reason seems to be that fear is a stronger emotion than avarice. Buyers push prices higher until they think that the price is no longer reasonable, and then they back away. On the other hand, sellers don't back away when prices drop—they dump their stock, exacerbating the drop.

COVERING SHORTS WHEN YOU ARE RIGHT

Since the usual decline is punctuated by a number of consolidations, and each of those consolidations comes after a power box to the downside, it is not always easy to know when to take the profits in a short position. The type of panic selling described previously is sometimes only the first of a number of selling binges. Therefore, it is often advisable to wait and see how the stock acts after the drop. A light-volume partial retracement of the drop is usually a sign that it was just a consolidation within a decline, and that the selling is not over. As we observed in selling out of long positions, when we are right we can be a little more patient and forgiving. Waiting to see if the consolidation after the decline is likely to hold can often add to profits.

In Figure 15.1 we see a stock that drops precipitously in just a few months. The first down-pointing arrow indicates the breakdown through support (horizontal line) which tells us to short the stock. The light-volume rally that follows is an ideal time to sell, as the price moves up almost to the breakdown level. After a long decline, we see three down arrows, each at a lower level and each indicating a very heavy volume week to the downside. Each looks like a climax low, but the first two are only temporary support prior to going lower. The last drop, however, is followed by a very square week on the downside and then a rally week that has immense volume but can not gain a commensurate advance. In the process, the descending trend is violated and the moving averages cross to the plus side. It looks at this point as though the decline is over, at least for the time being, and it is time to take profits.

Figure 15.1 **BOTTOMING—MORRISON KNUDSEN**

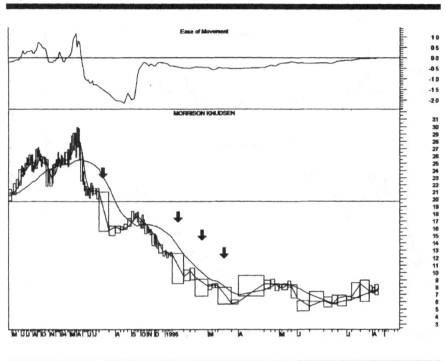

It would have been worthwhile to give the stock the benefit of the doubt on the earlier climactic postings and wait to see if the decline was really over. If the stock was shorted around the 20 level and dropped to the 10 area, a doubling of money, one could afford to watch and wait.

The more traditional type of bottoming is seen in Figure 15.2. The low is made on an extremely heavy posting and is well out of the bottom of the descending trend. Support comes in from there and is followed by a pullback on light volume about a month later. The turnaround is accompanied by a crossover on the moving average lines and is confirmed a bit later by the Ease of Movement. Notice that the volume on the final low is quite different from the volume on the con-

Figure 15.2 **BOTTOMING—SNAP-ON TOOLS**

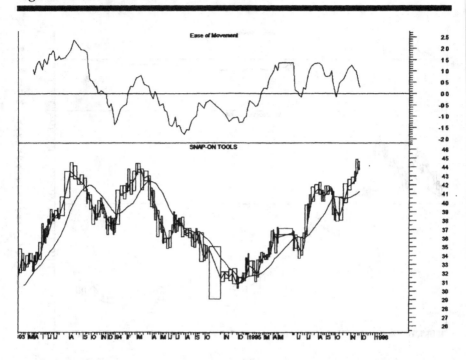

solidation that occurred halfway through the decline. On the final low, it remained heavy as the stock moved sideways. This is the same sort of action that we saw on many topping formations—we used it to distinguish between turning areas and resting areas.

COVERING SHORTS WHEN YOU ARE WRONG

Never stay wrong long. If a stock does not do what you expect it to do, get out of the position. Unlike the previous examples, in which there are good profits and the stock does pretty much as expected, there will be many times when the stock seems to follow all the rules, yet it does something unexpected after you short it. When that happens you should immediately cover the position and look for opportunities elsewhere. Let us look at a stock that looked perfect and then turned into a loser (Figure 15.3).

At the start of the chart, in mid-1994, Equifax was moving sideways within the range shown by the two horizontal lines. When it came down to that level in September, volume and trading range expanded, suggesting that downside pressure was coming in.

The rally into October produced a very square box at its conclusion, indicating resistance and telling us that the stock

Figure 15.3 **EQUIFAX**

wanted to go lower again. Then, in December, we saw the big down box designated by a down arrow. Aha! A power box to the downside through the old support, and the moving averages had even gone to the sell side. The stock looked like an ideal short.

Holding the short position through the next few weeks, it looked as though the position would work out well. Volume decreased as the price moved somewhat higher—a typical consolidation after a breakdown. But suddenly the stock leapt higher, as indicated by the up arrow. It became obvious that something was wrong. The volume took it above the previous rally high, the moving averages crossed back to the buy side, and the down pattern was destroyed. No amount of wishful thinking could get around the fact that the stock was acting wrong. At that point it needed to be covered.

There is no reason, in such a case, to wait and hope. This is just one example, but anytime a situation acts in such a way as to negate the original reason for entering it, it should be eliminated.

THE FEAR SYNDROME

We spoke in prior chapters about the danger of letting emotions warp our judgment. There is, perhaps, no greater pitfall than being an adamant and continuing bear. Very often, the problem stems from the fact that bad news sells. Whether in an advisory letter, a television program, or a newspaper, it is the dire forecast that gets the attention of the public. Books that forecast disaster sell better than those that forecast prosperity. I have a bookshelf with a number of books that all forecast doom, all written at different times—none of them have yet come true. That is not to say that they will *always* be wrong, but it is a real danger to look for disaster so constantly as to miss opportunities.

We can make money on the short side of the market by realistically observing stocks and markets that are turning lower. We cannot, however, always remain short, believing that someday the crash will come. A trader who is filled with a fear of the future is likely to overstay bad positions, believing that disaster is just around the corner. Since we know the news is selling us fear, we must at least counteract that fear with realism, if not with optimism. If a short position goes bad, as in the earlier example, it should be eliminated.

I remember another broker's customer who was short through much of the 1970 to 1972 bull market. He could, and did, tell anyone who would listen all the reasons why the market was too high. After a great number of margin calls, he finally threw in the towel and covered the shorts near the end of 1972. In 1973, the market started an 18-month decline—but by then he was out of the market, a good deal poorer than when he started.

Other Markets

If it is a traded market for which the information is available, then Equivolume, Ease of Movement, and Volume Adjusted Moving Averages can all be used effectively. Sometimes, the trick is getting the information, especially when dealing with foreign markets. In recent years there has been a move to make a good deal more data available, but in many cases there is a long way to go.

FUTURES

In Figure 16.1, we see that the Equivolume methodology is very effective in a futures contract. Notice particularly the power box on the first day of April. It takes the price up through the resistance that has held it back since the middle of February. It is the heaviest volume seen on the chart to that time—a strong signal to buy. Just as we saw in stocks, the breakout is followed by a light-volume pullback before the price moves higher—another opportunity to buy.

Later, toward the end of April, there is another power box to the upside, as the February high is decisively penetrated. Also, as on a stock chart, the pullbacks tend to be on decreasing volume, followed by heavy volume on the resumption of the advance.

Figure 16.1 **LIGHT CRUDE**

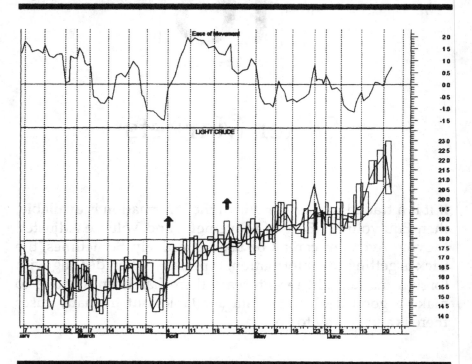

There are a few differences between stocks and futures contracts that should be taken into consideration. Futures contracts have a limited life, with no volume or open interest when they first start to trade, then building to high numbers as they near delivery date, and finally disappearing at delivery. That distorts the volume figures for a single contract— May wheat, for example. The best way to cope with this is to chart the price of the contract being traded, but use the volume figure for *all* contracts. In that way the aberrations based upon the age of the contract tend to be smoothed out, producing a usable Equivolume chart. So, you would chart the price for May wheat, but use the volume for all the wheat contracts in the market.

Commodities also have trading limits. If a predetermined price move is exceeded, trading is halted—thereby distorting both price and volume. Often this results in gaps—and square days on an Equivolume chart. There is no real way to cope with this, except to be aware of it and take it into consideration when studying the chart. It is not usually a major problem and should not deter you from using Equivolume charts in trading futures contracts.

Let us look at another futures contract, for 30-year Treasury Bonds (Figure 16.2). These are daily postings covering about six months of history. The down arrow points to the power box to the downside that broke support and started the month-long slide. That is followed by an upward power box

Figure 16.2 **TREASURY BONDS**

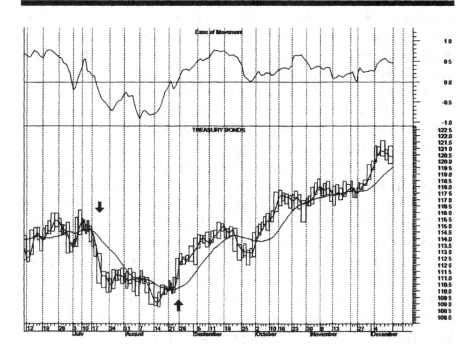

in late August, indicated by the up-pointing arrow, which is the start of a very substantial advance as interest rates drop. We see here that the Ease of Movement is also very helpful, crossing negative early in the decline and then going back to the plus side in conjunction with the power box up. The two moving average lines are similarly informative, crossing in a very timely fashion.

STOCK MARKET FUTURES

A special case is the trading of futures contracts, such as the Standard & Poor's (S&P) contract, which are based upon an underlying index. Not only is the Equivolume work helpful, but short-term applications of the Arms Index can provide an exciting technical tool. With the leverage provided by the futures market, combined with the accessible information on volume, this market can be very rewarding. Of course, the additional rewards offered by leverage carry with them a commensurate additional risk. It is a two-edged sword.

To trade market futures I look at the market itself, rather than the futures contract. The contract moves in response to the market, and the market average and volume are less erratic numbers. Of course, the price of the contract is important in the actual trading, since it tends to oscillate above and below its fair value, but I prefer to use the underlying market and the overall market statistics in making the decisions that lead up to the actual trading. In Figure 16.3 we see seven months of trading in 1994. This is really too long a time period to look at if one is trading, but here it allows us to see a number of market swings, in order to understand the technique. In actual trading, I would look at the last two months or so. In that way every small move is apparent, and small moves are big profits or losses in trading market futures.

Figure 16.3 **NYSE COMPOSITE**

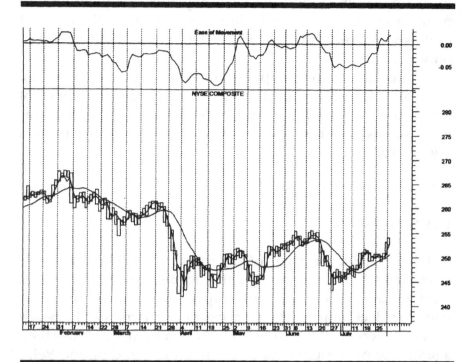

Particularly noticeable on this chart is that tops tend to have square postings, whereas lows tend to have climactic action. In addition, we see that volume tends to get heavier on declines in the first part of the chart, but then volume is heavier on up days in the second half of the chart. The dividing line is the beginning of April, when the climactic low is made after the sharp decline. All these features are similar to what we learned about individual issues. The combination of volume and price spread tells us where prices are likely to go. Also look at the Ease of Movement, which is very effective in finding the turning points, although there are a couple of whipsaws in April and May. And the two moving average lines are extremely informative. They cross early enough, in most cases, to allow profitable trades. We are talking about quite short-term positions. Some last a month, but most last only a few days.

Although many people trade these contracts on an extremely short-term basis, sometimes doing a number of round turns in a single day, I trade the time frame that this work seems to be best for—positions that last a few days to a few weeks.

THE ARMS INDEX

In tandem with the chart of the market, I look at the short-term Arms Index numbers. It should be stressed that actual numbers are not as important as apparent extremes. In a sideways or declining market, an extremely overbought 5-day moving average of the AI is likely to be a higher number than a similarly overbought condition in an uptrending market. I try to compare the current level to other readings seen over the last few cycles and look at the market to try to ascertain the trend. If it is obviously a very strong up trend, I do not expect to see such oversold levels on the pullbacks and do expect to see more extreme overbought levels on the tops.

Figure 16.4 illustrates the swings in the 5-day Arms Index during the time frame covered by the market chart in Figure 16.3. It should be apparent by comparing dates that high points on the 5-day AI coincide very nicely with low points on the market, and vice versa. There are three prominent peaks on the AI, all of which could have been used as buy signals with profitable results. Also, there are two prominent low points on the AI, which could have been used as signals to sell, and each would have been close to the top of the move. Using these signals, one does not trade, signal to signal, how-

Figure 16.4 **5-DAY ARMS INDEX—JANUARY–JULY, 1994**

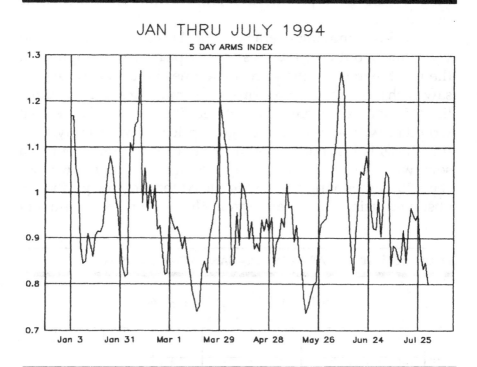

JAN THRU JULY 1994

5 DAY ARMS INDEX

ever. Moves tend to develop quite fast, so the best strategy is usually to act on the Arms Index extreme but cover the position when the move appears to be losing its momentum on the Equivolume chart. It does not take big moves to make money in futures contracts and waiting for the next signal very often allows a large part of the profit to be erased. In addition, as in any trading, if the market does not act as expected, the losing position should be eliminated as soon as the error becomes apparent.

There are a number of lesser peaks and troughs on the 5-day chart that could also be used as trading signals. A trader who wants to make more than a few trades in a six-month

time frame might wish to watch and use those also. Most of
them would have produced a profit in the illustrated time
period.

The 5-day moving average of the AI is very sensitive, and
very timely, but it produces so many peaks and troughs that
the most extreme signals are sometimes hard to spot. As we
saw with the longer-term Arms Index moving averages, timeliness is not greatly harmed by extending the time frame, as it
would be with a moving average of price. Consequently, little
timeliness is lost but smoothing is gained by going out to a
somewhat longer-term moving average. In Figure 16.5, we
see a 10-day moving average of the AI for the time period we
observed using the 5-day. Again, there are three prominent

Figure 16.5 **10-DAY ARMS INDEX—JANUARY–JULY, 1994**

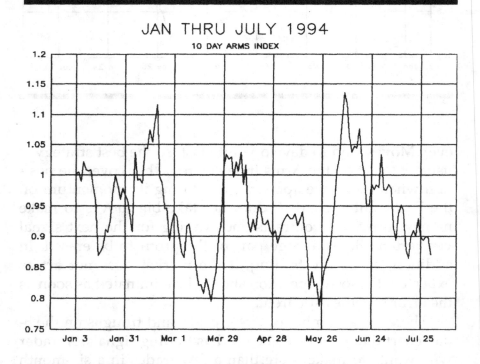

peaks and two troughs. The troughs still coincide with market tops, and the peaks coincide with market bottoms rather well. We have gained readability without losing timeliness. We have, however, eliminated a number of secondary signals that a more aggressive trader could have used. I suggest following the index on both bases and—as always—watching the market with the Equivolume chart.

The preceding is not a mechanical system, nor should it be reduced to one. Every trade is a judgment, weighing the market and the Arms Index information. One way to be less inclined to move too soon is to wait for a reversal in the Arms Index moving average rather than try to act when it seems to be at an extreme. Especially when selling an overbought market, what appears to be an extreme in the Arms Index can become even more extreme. Since tops tend to roll over, I like to see rolling over in the AI moving average and sell short just when it starts to go toward higher numbers. On the other end of the spectrum, when it gives oversold numbers, there is more hurry to act, because the turn can come off a sharp down point very rapidly. Oversold extremes tend more to be precise points rather than areas.

For the short-term aggressive trader who likes the leverage and excitement of futures, the combination of Arms Index and Equivolume provides a way to use market index futures to trade systematically and unemotionally. It is not for the faint-hearted, and certainly is not for persons who are unable to separate themselves from their fear and greed.

Conclusions

I find it interesting that I have never seen two stock charts that are exactly alike. They may appear to be very similar, especially if they are two similar companies, in the same industry, and over the same period of history, but there are still many differences in their behavior. Even market averages, which smooth out and merge together a great number of issues, do not repeat their patterns exactly. In the early chapters we looked at a century of market history and found many similarities, but there are no two historical periods in which the market has done exactly the same thing. The market is very complex. It is pushed one way or the other in varying degrees as a result of the individual decisions of millions of participants. Some of those participants are acting logically and others are acting emotionally, and each is having an effect proportional to the money involved. With so many variables, it is little wonder that every chart is unique.

Yet, we have spent 16 chapters trying to find similarities that can help us make money. We can do that because the emotional responses of people are repetitive, in spite of the infinite number of fundamental forces that can affect a stock. Fear and greed are always operative in the market, and their effects are visible and predictable. A stock makes a head and shoulders top because fear usually takes over from greed in a gradual manner. On the other hand, lows tend to be very sharp because fear eventually leads to panic and indiscriminate dumping. The exact configuration of the chart in either case is never the same twice, but the emotional response and the general pattern are evident and recognizable.

The usual bar charts ignore volume, and in that way simplify the picture. No two bar charts really look the same either, but they tend to be more alike than Equivolume charts, which include the additional variable of volume. It is the volume that gives us the real picture of the emotions in the marketplace. Price tells us *what* is happening, but volume tells us *how* it is happening. With Equivolume we create a more complex picture, but a more informative picture.

This is not a trading *system* we have been studying, but a trading *discipline*. A system is based upon immutable rules—a certain number or action demands a preset response. Such a simple solution is not compatible with anything as complex as the stock or commodities markets. It takes the reasoning ability of a human brain to cope with the complexity and recognize the similarities that are hidden within the diversity. I said earlier that the modern trader must use a computer just to stay competitive. That is true, but the computer can only present the data in as understandable a form as possible. Individual judgment cannot be relegated to a computer: It is the responsibility of the trader.

The only way to know what to expect in the future is to understand the past. Therefore, I like to look back at markets and stocks over many years of history. I find that prices and names change, but patterns stay very similar. In 1932 or 1966 people reacted emotionally to news items and economic developments just as they do today. The news and the economy are different, but human emotional responses remain the same. The early market history charts in this book came from an inexpensive historical data service on CD-ROM disks provided quarterly by Momentum Enterprises of Charlotte, North Carolina. I am also able, using these disks, to look at thousands of individual stocks over many years of history. It is a worthwhile exercise to study charts from other times and realize that the rules never change, just the participants.

The markets—whether stock, futures, currencies, or bonds; whether domestic or foreign—move because of human emotions. Certainly, there are fundamental forces behind those emotions, but no fundamental factor can affect price until it has been evaluated and responded to by a human brain (or a computer that was programmed by a human). The final result of the filtering and evaluation is seen in the price and volume. They are the distillation of every action—logical or illogical, emotional or unemotional—that creates buying and selling pressures. I believe that the objective trader who observes those emotions rather than succumbing to them is the trader who succeeds. Equivolume, Ease of Movement, Volume Adjusted Moving Averages, and the Arms Index are tools that can lead to that objectivity and that success.

Index

in bull markets, 118
causes of, 168–169
and decline, termination of, 197
for short sales, 189
and tops, 125
in a volume breakout, 148,
150–153
price, 217
and emotionalism, 12, 216
and sell decisions, 174
price movements, 9
of commodities, 207
and Equivolume charting, 23–26
and greed, 11
as market bottoms, 127
and short sales, 195–196
smoothing, with moving
averages, 51
tides, gauging, 79–83
and trading range, 36
and trading success, 23–24
trends and 3-VAMA, 104
profits
average per trade, 47
and base, size of, 175
in bull markets, 78–79
and Ease of Movement parameters, 97–99
end of decline, 198
for market futures, 211–212
and optimizing Ease of Movement, 45–48
and power boxes, 148, 150–153
and price movements, 24
and resistance levels, 29
in rising market, 76–78, 181–182
and sell decisions, 174
speed of advance, 188
at tops, 182–183
trending markets, 61–62

pullback lows, investing during,
147, 153
pullbacks, 28–29
in bull markets, 117
and completing the buy, 153,
158, 165–166, 171
on daily charts, 165
late in bull market, 157
after a market decline, 146
market trends, 83
puts, during downside reversals,
189–190

Quinn, Edwin S., 34

rallies
base of, 118, 144
in bear markets, 121
in bull markets, 117
of downside reversals, 189
to a high, 156
market trends, 83
and short sales, timing of, 196
in a volume breakout, 150
resistance
and Equivolume boxes, 29,
92–93
and power boxes, 148
and tops, 123–124
upside, 32–33
resting phases, 113, 121
and sell decisions, 180
reversals, 113–115, 122
downside, 189–190
and market futures, 213
moving average signals, 133
ripples, 73
risk
estimating, with Arms Index, 16
of leverage, 208

risk *(continued)*
  reducing, 122
  reducing, with diversification,
    171–172
  roll overs, downside, 3, 189–191
  runaway gaps, 93
  of short sales, 187, 194–195

St. Jude Medical, charting,
    165–168
sell decisions
  Arms Index and, 185
  for bad positions, 184–186
  consolidations, based on, 179–
    183
  and monitoring positions, 174–
    179
  objectivity of, 186
sell signals, 191, 193
  on charts, 105
  for longer-term EOM, 100
  for market futures, 210–212
  and smoothed moving averages,
    53
short sales, 76, 187–196
  in bear market rally, 158
  chart pattern for, 189
  consolidations, monitoring, 192
  covering positions, 198–202
  emotionalism of, 186
  at end of advance, 182
  of market futures, 213
  method of, 195–196
  risks of, 187–188
  timing of, 194–195
short-term positions, and market
    futures, 210
Short Term Trading Index, 16, 131.
    See also Arms Index
sideways movement, 10
  and market trends, 83

moving averages for, 104
and reversals, 114–115
and sell decisions, 180, 183
and tops, 124
and whipsaws, 41
smoothing
  of Arms Index, 135–139
  of Ease of Movement, 40–44
  timeliness of signals, 42–43, 53
speculation
  in bear market rallies, 144
  and short selling, 188–189
spread, and box ratios, 36–37
Standard & Poor's (S&P) con-
    tracts, trading of, 208–210
standoff market, 10
  Arms Index of, 17
stock index, and the Arms Index,
    132–133
stocks
  base of, 175–176
  buying, 161–172
  charts of, 10–11
  cycles, 107–111, 177–179
  and Ease of Movement, 97
  Equivolume boxes, shape of,
    24–27
  and gaps, 93–94
  long-term moves, 164
  monitoring, 173–174
  movement and Equivolume
    charting, 26
  price of, 12
  requirements for a buy, 33
  short-term positions, 147
  sideways movement, 40
  strength, signs of, 29–30
  technical analysis of, 11
  trading, after market decline,
    144
  trading, in trends, 97